LETTER FROM NEW YORK

BBC Woman's Hour Broadcasts

ALSO BY HELENE HANFF

Apple of My Eye

The Duchess of Bloomsbury Street

84, Charing Cross Road

Q's Legacy

Underfoot in Show Business

LETTER
from
NEW YORK

Helene Hanff

HarperPerennial
A Division of HarperCollins*Publishers*

HarperCollins books may be purchased for educational, business, or sales promotional use. For information please write: Special Markets Department, HarperCollins Publishers, Inc., 10 East 53rd Street, New York, NY 10022.

LIBRARY OF CONGRESS CATALOG CARD NUMBER 92-54842
ISBN 0-06-097543-1

93 94 95 96 97 RRD 10 9 8 7 6 5 4 3 2

TO:

Chris Longley, who hired me;

Sue MacGregor, who "presented" me;

Ursula Kenny, who "produced" me in New York;

And all the other lovely people at BBC's Woman's Hour.

With much gratitude and affection.

AUTHOR'S NOTE

In the summer of 1978, I had dinner in London with my friend Chris Longley who had just been made a producer on the popular BBC radio magazine, the "Woman's Hour."

"How would you feel," she asked me tentatively, "about broadcasting a five-minute talk for us once a month?"

"What would I talk about?" I asked.

"Your life in New York," said Chris. "I love the stories you tell me—about the dogs in your building, your neighborhood, Central Park. We see photographs of skyscraper apartment houses. We can't visualize people living in them. I want you to talk about your everyday life to the "Woman's Hour" audience just the way you talk about it to me. Could you do that?"

"I don't see why not," I said.

"Five minutes, once a month," Chris repeated. "The Powers-That-Be are willing to try it for six months."

"So am I," I said.

The six months turned out to be six years. Then I went off the air. I filed the manila envelope with its accumulation of two-and-a-half page scripts in my storage cabinet. There it sat until the summer of '91 when—*apropos* of I can't imagine what—I mentioned the broadcasts to Jennifer Moyer. She immediately asked if she could read the scripts, and when she'd read them, she passed them on to her husband and publishing partner, Britt Bell.

The next day a beautiful flowering plant arrived with a note:

"Britt and I love the scripts! May we make them into a book?"

Reading the scripts for the first time, I discovered that a few of them had gone missing over the years. The rest are offered here in the hope that they will pass an hour pleasantly for you .

NINETEEN SEVENTY-EIGHT

1978

OCTOBER

You have no idea what it's like here in October. You'd have to live through three months of the soggy ninety-degree heat of a New York summer to know how it feels when you wake up one morning and it's suddenly fall.

And you walk down Fifth Avenue on a Saturday, smelling the chestnuts roasting and the hot pretzels at every corner stand, and you look at the new fall clothes in the windows of Bergdorf's and Bonwit's and Saks. And your tongue hangs out to buy one of the new pantsuits to wear to Connecticut or wherever, when you drive up "to see the leaves."

Every October New Yorkers suddenly become nature lovers. Everybody finds a friend with a car, and the whole town drives somewhere in the country to see the leaves. Paul, our Yugoslav doorman, told me our American autumn foliage is world-famous; it doesn't exist anywhere else in the world. He met some Japanese who'd saved up for years to make the trip to see a New England autumn.

I'll tell you what it's like. We drove up to Bear Mountain last year, and the whole side of the mountain looked as if a house-painter had thrown buckets of paint at it. Not just red and orange and yellow, but blue and lavender. You look at the colors of the leaves and you don't believe them.

Even in Central Park you'll see flaming red and orange trees—and a yellow that on a grey day looks lit by a 500-watt bulb. So after you've done Fifth Avenue you walk home through the park. It's full of fat, bushy, grey squirrels waiting for a last load of peanuts to bury for the winter. If you have no peanuts, they'll settle for lollipops. They don't bury those, they eat them while you wait. They sit bolt upright on their hind paws and peel the lollipops carefully with their front paws and eat them peck-peck-peck, like a woodpecker.

When you get home, you go round to the supermarket and you know it's election season. There'll be a flock of young candidates outside the market to shake your hand and give you fliers about themselves, and tell you what nothing local office they're running for. And please don't just vote for governor and go home, they know it's a long ballot but the offices lower down do matter, so please don't forget to vote for them—on the bottom line of a fourteen-line ballot.

And you come home and make the season's first hot chili and the season's first applesauce to cool off the chili. And if you live in my building, you put on a sweater at ten-thirty or eleven p.m. and go round the block with the building's dogs and dog owners. I go around the block with Richard, who owns an Old English sheepdog named Chester, and Nina, who owns a worried-looking German shepherd named Duke. Walking around our block in October, you know this is moving-and-housecleaning season. You'll see a pile of furniture some family threw out, standing by the gutter waiting for the Sanitation Department. And somebody'll say, "If you sanded that table down to the natural wood . . ." or "That's a perfectly good lamp; if you just put new wiring . . ."

We had a super in our building named Leo, who ran a regular Macy's basement down in our cellar storeroom, with the furniture tenants left behind. He'd fix the broken lamps and tables, and his wife would clean the sofas and armchairs, and tenants would run down to the storeroom and look everything over, and haggle. . . .

And you come home and have coffee and homemade chocolate cake up in Nina's penthouse and come down to your own place and go to bed, sleeping under blankets for the first time in months. And when the alarm goes off at seven a.m., you're shot out of a cannon, panting to get to work on your new book. And you want to clean the closets and buy a new rug for the bathroom, because January First is a delusion. The New Year begins in October, when New York is suddenly alive and jumping with new Broadway shows and new books in the bookstores and a new Philharmonic season and new restaurants opening and everybody moves quickly, everybody makes plans, there are new worlds to conquer and anything can happen.

NOVEMBER

Before the days of James the First, a group of English farmers disagreed with the Church of England. "They will conform," said King James, "or I will harry them out of the kingdom." They didn't conform, and he harried them out of the kingdom. They got on a ship called the *Mayflower* and sailed to the New World, and landed at Plymouth, Massachusetts, and established a colony. And since they called themselves "pilgrims" they became known to American history as the Pilgrim Fathers.

Now frankly, they were no better than they should be. Driven out of England for refusing to conform to the Church of England, they promptly drove out of Plymouth all who refused to conform to the Church of Plymouth. Never mind: they gave us a lovely American holiday.

What happened was: the Pilgrims were befriended by the

native Americans—the Indians—who taught them how to fertilize the land with eels, how to grow Indian corn and eat it off the cob, and how to cook and eat an American bird called a turkey. And the next autumn, when the Pilgrims reaped a bountiful harvest, they invited the Indians to a feast where everybody gave thanks to God for the harvest. That feast was the first American Thanksgiving.

Thanksgiving Day is the fourth Thursday in November, the whole country shuts down for it—and a Pilgrim would have a heart attack if he could see how it's celebrated, especially in New York, New York. What makes New York's Thanksgiving unique, is the Macy Parade, which has been hauling parents out of bed early on Thanksgiving Day for fifty-five years. The parade features helium-filled balloon likenesses of cartoon characters, each as tall as a six- or seven-story building.

It is therefore the only parade that floats high above the street—Central Park West—and is watched by huge crowds all staring upward. Enterprising mothers will spend several hours on the telephone, several days ahead of time, to wangle invitations from friends who live in Central Park West apartment houses, to bring the children over to watch the parade from their windows—which may be level with, or slightly above or below, the towering, inflated balloon figures of Mickey Mouse, Snoopy and Big Bird sailing by.

There are church services on Thanksgiving morning and while Grandma is at church and Mom is already in the kitchen squaring off for Thanksgiving dinner, Dad is digging out his old college pennant, booster button and varsity sweater, in preparation for the afternoon football game. Thanksgiving marks the end of the college football season, and the Thanksgiving Day game—like your Oxford-Cambridge boat race—takes place year after year between the same university rivals. The most famous of these rivalries is that of the two service colleges—the U.S. Military Academy at West Point, New York, and the U.S. Naval Academy at Annapolis, Maryland. In alternate years when the game is at West Point—a short drive for New Yorkers up to Bear Mountain—New York City swarms with young Army and Navy cadets in their dashing uniforms.

After the football game, the young generation repairs to college fraternity houses for the victory parties, which take place even if your team lost 50 to 0. And Dad drives home to see to the drinks that precede Thanksgiving dinner, itself usually a duplicate of Christmas dinner, from the turkey and cranberry sauce to the pumpkin and apple pies. But the table decorations are pure Thanksgiving, featuring the bright orange-and-brown ears of Indian corn, inedible and never seen at any other time.

Everybody will make pigs of themselves at dinner, since lunch was either a hot dog and container of coffee at the stadium, or a sandwich eaten in front of the TV set watching at least three college football games, in a country with so many time zones that an East Coast game is ending just as a West Coast game begins.

But the real hallmark of Thanksgiving is the homecoming of family members living, or working, or going to college far from home. Even though many of them will have to be back at their jobs on Friday, Americans across the country are determined to get home for Thanksgiving, our quintessential family holiday, more so even than Christmas, since it embraces all religions and recalls the Dissenters' faith on which this country was founded. So every fourth Thursday in November, I lift a martini glass in salute to Samoset and the Pilgrims, who gave us the warmest homecoming holiday ever Made in America.

DECEMBER

This is the season when there are two kinds of New Yorkers: those who hate-the-holidays and flee them on some cruise ship; and those who look forward to them as passionately as any five-year-old. To a passionate five-year-old like me, Christmas in New York has dazzling advantages. But celebrating it properly in a New York "studio" apartment—a one-room flat—has disadvantages that would drive any house owner clear up the wall. We'll take the advantages first.

Christmas in New York begins with the Park Avenue tree-lighting ceremony up at the Brick Presbyterian church. I have to explain first of all that our Avenues run through the island from south to north, and are intersected by the Streets which run east to west; and second, Park Avenue gets its name from the strip of green grass and flower beds running down the middle of it from 96th Street to 45th. Well, at Christmas, a small evergreen tree is set up at every second street along the Avenue's green strip and is decorated only with small white-gold lights. On the appointed day, you go up to the church at 94th and Park, to an outdoor carol service; and the minister or somebody pulls a switch and you see the lights come on, on all the little trees, clear down the Avenue for fifty blocks.

That's my signal to go shopping—and Christmas shopping on Fifth Avenue is full of lovely diversions. First you queue up at Lord & Taylor's to see their Christmas windows. This year's windows feature Coming Home for Christmas. One window has a replica of a JFK airport terminal, complete with life-like passengers, luggage and waiting room. Another has a replica of the George Washington Bridge, with the lights, the traffic—and a hapless driver stuck with a flat tire. My favorite window has a replica of a New York subway station, with crowds, a snack bar and a gent coming down the steps with a Christmas tree over his shoulder.

If you're shopping on a Wednesday, you drop in, at noon, at St. Thomas's church—halfway between Saks and Bonwit's—to hear their marvelous men's and boys' choirs do Benjamin Britten's *St. Nicholas* or the *Ceremony of Carols*. And of course you stop at Rockefeller Plaza at twilight, for the carol singing under the sixty-five-foot-high Christmas tree.

The free concerts here in December are wonderful altogether. Each week you read the Sunday church notices in the *Times* and make agonizing decisions. Should you chase all the way up to Riverside church at 122nd Street to hear the best *Messiah* in town—or settle for a Bach Christmas oratorio at St. Bartholomew's at 49th and Park? And if you do hear Bach at St. Bart's this Sunday, will you get the best *Messiah* next Sunday down at Ascension at Tenth Street or up at Heavenly Rest at 94th Street?

If you're at an evening concert in midtown, you walk home up Park Avenue afterwards. Midtown Park Avenue is lined with skyscraper office towers, set in landscaped plazas; and at Christmas, the shrubs in the plazas are strung with tiny white lights, mere pinpricks of light, but thousands of them. You walk home between aisles of ground-level stars with the gold-lit trees running up the middle.

My own tree goes up the Saturday night before Christmas, but I don't have my annual tree trimming party any more. Which brings us to the problems of a one-room Christmas. In this age of sofa beds, it is my belief that the real reason for the existence of bedrooms is to have a place to put guests' coats. The day of my tree trimming party, I used to carry my entire wardrobe up to a friend's bedroom-apartment, to make room in my double-door closet for twenty-five guests' coats. I'd invite the twenty-five active members of my Democratic Club to the party; and if a few singles said, "Can I bring somebody?" I'd say, "Sure." I'd get eight or ten regrets and invite eight or ten more people from a neighboring Democratic

Club. Well, one year there was a blizzard, everybody who was going away stayed home, and forty-two people came to my party. I ran out of food, forks and floor space, and at midnight the closet rack fell down from the weight of forty-two winter coats, and that was the end of my annual tree trimming party.

I have eight people and two dogs coming for Christmas dinner and since studio apartments have small refrigerators, you have to work out the logistics in advance. You make your pies, cranberry sauce and sweet-potato casserole ahead of time and then distribute them around the building in other people's refrigerators, since the turkey, hors d'oeuvres, vegetables and eggnog bowl are all you'll have room for in yours. On Christmas morning once your turkey's in the oven, you go and get everything back. And the logistics consists in remembering whether the casserole is in 4-F or 16-B, and did you get the keys to 8-E-up-the-hall, because Shelley and Susan have gone skiing in Vermont for Christmas, with your pies in their freezer.

Duke, the German shepherd, comes to Christmas dinner, Chester, the Old English sheepdog, comes for dessert and coffee, and I haven't filled their Christmas stockings yet. I'm going over to Saks' Dog Shop to see what's new. My high-fashion friend, Arlene, phoned to say she got her presents for the two dogs there.

"It's a canine aftershave called Sniffe. S-n-i-f-f-e. Is that *chic*?!"

Merry Christmas.

NINETEEN SEVENTY-NINE

1979

JANUARY

This is the month when I sit at my typewriter by the window on a raw, sleeting morning, and stare down with pity at all the office-slaves huddled under the bus shelter across the street, eight floors below. In any season, I wouldn't trade their steady salaries and pensions for the privilege of working at home but especially I wouldn't trade in January. Our building is a cozy rabbit-warren to hibernate in, but on the winter evening when you feel you've *got* to get out of the house, you only go a block or two to find what you crave.

Within two square blocks of my building, you have a choice of three Chinese restaurants, two Italian, two Czech, two French, one Indian, one Cuban, two seafood restaurants, two steak houses, three hamburger joints, and two deli restaurants. After dinner, within two blocks, there's the Phoenix, an off-Broadway theatre with Broadway standards (Alec McCowen's *Gospel According to St. Mark* was done there); there's LOOM, the Light Opera of Manhattan, which does Gilbert & Sullivan and *The Merry Widow*; there's a Workshop Theatre, two movie houses and three discotheques.

For ordinary everyday living, you need go no further than around the corner to the supermarket, or across the street to the cleaners, the drug store (chemist's to you), the liquor store (off-license) and the deli. If you're sick, they all deliver. Otherwise, the building is self-sufficient, with its own mailbox and a laundry in the basement.

I take my wash down early in the morning and then ride up to the lobby mailroom to pick up the mail and admire the red wool coats, green turtleneck sweaters and plaid raincoats of all the short-haired dogs coming in from their morning walk. And I stop to read all the hand-lettered notices on the bulletin board:

"Baby carriage for sale. Will take first fair offer." They'll take the first offer because our baby-carriage-and-bicycle room is crowded, and an unused carriage gets banged up in there.

"Reliable baby sitter, lives in building. Phone after school." She's sixteen and she's earning money to buy a guitar.

"Sofa bed and dinette set. Like new." The model on the sixth floor is getting married.

Paul, one of our doormen, has a sign up, advertising his car-and-driver services. In summer on his days off, Paul drives old ladies to the seashore; and all year round he drives everybody to the airport. Now he's branching out. He's got a ski rack on his car and he'll drive skiers to New England instead of the airport.

Afternoons I take Duke, Nina's German shepherd, to Central Park for an hour, especially if there's snow. There's a broad sloping hill at our entrance; and by common consent, the sledders take the near side of the hill and the skiers take the far side, leaving a middle aisle for dogs to chase sticks, or just roll downhill in the snow, which Duke does with ecstasy. At the bottom of the hill, children ice-skate on the Model Sailboat Pond, and the whole scene looks like a Grandma Moses Christmas card. But we're five long blocks from the park, and in bitter weather when there's no snow to lure me, it's hard to make myself go. I go for Duke's sake—and because it feels so good to come home afterward, to thrust your feet into furry slippers, cup your frozen hands round a mug of hot coffee, feel the rush of heat in the pipes as darkness closes in, and know why T.S. Eliot wrote: "Winter kept us warm."

Evening is when all the drama happens around here. There was the night when Mr. Shulman, aged ninety-one, suddenly appeared in the lobby in his pajamas at two a.m. and then went wandering down Second Avenue looking for somebody who could sing him the words to "It Might As Well Be Spring." A young couple coming in late chased after him and brought him home. Then there was the dinner-hour when old Mrs. Miller, who lived across the hall from me, got her hand caught in the mail chute. She was in her eighties and she had swollen arthritic fingers, so Murphy, the doorman on duty, borrowed my olive oil and poured a little of it over her fingers to work them loose. The next morning I had to lurk around the lobby mailbox at collection time to see how many letters had got smeared up. And there was the night the Siamese cat got on the elevator by himself, causing a seventeen-story building-wide hunt for him at ten p.m.

Night is also the time when you come down with something. The winter I had the flu, everybody on my floor offered to do my marketing and my laundry and pick up my mail; Nina—Duke's mother—positively drowned me in homemade soup and Chester, the old English sheepdog, paid a sick call wearing a Red Cross cap and a stethoscope, borrowed by Schor, the actor, from a theatrical props department. Last small town in America.

FEBRUARY

If you try to visualize New Yorkers' homes by looking at the skyline, you'll think we all live in cubbyholes on the forty-seventh floor of a skyscraper. But two thirds of the skyline is made up of office buildings; and since New York is a string of neighborhoods totally unlike each other, each neighborhood determines the size of people's homes and the way they're furnished.

In Greenwich Village, for instance, few people live in tall buildings. Most Villagers live in three- or four-story walk-ups. No elevators and no incinerators, which means they don't put their garbage down a chute in the hall to be burned up. They put it on the sidewalk or in the back alley, to be picked up—at three or four a.m.—by the noisy sanitation trucks whose racket we all learn to sleep through.

Generally speaking, Village flats have two or three small rooms; decor, cheerfully Bohemian. Bright woven Mexican rugs, lots of orange and yellow cushions, abstract wall paintings by Village artists, pottery ashtrays, vases and coffee mugs made in Village shops. The furniture is painted wood, the makeshift bookshelves have books on astrology, psychotherapy and health food cookery: how to make tofu hamburgers, how to combine three kinds of beans for protein so you can live without meat from nastily slaughtered animals.

Upper Park Avenue is three express subway stops from the Village—and light-years away in atmosphere. Park Avenue apartment houses are old, solid brown stone and owned by their tenants. The apartments take up a whole floor or a half a floor; each has a large foyer, a living room, dining room, several bedrooms and a maid's room or a maid's-and-butler's suite. Each has a back door, a service entrance next to the kitchen. The living room is full of antiques, Oriental rugs and period furniture; the wall paintings are Old Masters; the books are sets of classics in glass-doored bookcases and look as if they've never been read. But the buildings are old, which means they were built before air conditioners, laundry machines or dishwashers, all of which must be installed by the tenants who want them. My friend and editor Gene Young told me her mother sold her Park Avenue apartment and moved into a modern building. Now Gene's mother, Juliana Young, had been the first protocol officer of the UN and the personification of the diplomatic service in Old China. "And the only thing she misses is the service entrance," said Gene. "She *dies* of shame at having to carry her garbage through the living room and out the front door to the hall incinerator."

The Upper West Side is another neighborhood of old brownstone apartment houses with large five- and six-room apartments. Anne Jackson and Eli Wallach have raised three children in one on Riverside Drive where they've lived for the past thirty years. It's furnished in middle-class family style: an old piano, old mahogany dining room suite, old sofas and overstuffed chairs. Upper West Side kitchens are large and airy and, to an Upper *East* Sider equipped with horrendous ancient stoves and ancient sinks with iron pipes showing. The bathrooms are also large and airy with ancient, pock-marked bathtubs and sinks yellowed and age-stained.

So come on over to the Upper East Side, to Third Avenue or Second or First, where the high-rise apartment houses are less than thirty years old, air-conditioning is built in, the incinerator's down the hall, the laundry's in the basement and people do live in cubbyholes. (Except those like Richard Nixon, who can pay two thousand a month just to maintain the twelve-room apartment they've already bought for one million eight hundred thousand dollars.)

Most East Siders are middle-income working people who live in one-room apartments, or have a living room and one bedroom, except for the working-class rich in top-floor penthouses. Pianos have to be raised on outdoor pulleys and eased in through your tenth-floor window, since the elevators and front doors are too small for them. The bathrooms are even smaller, or, as a gentleman once remarked of my bathroom: "If three people want to stand in it, two of them better be in love." Department stores sell nylon shag bathroom carpeting for East Siders, and the largest size they carry is four feet by six. I bought my tearose-pink bathroom carpeting in the three-by-five size, knowing it was too big, so that after my friend Richard cut it to fit the floor, he had enough left over to cover the entire toilet tank.

East Side kitchens are just as small but with shiny modern stoves, sinks and refrigerators and—in bedroom apartments—dishwashers. But any West Sider would be appalled to watch me prepare a full turkey dinner on one small tabletop or to discover that neither my bathroom nor my kitchen has a window; they have blinding fluorescent lights instead and ventilators that don't work.

Arlene's 8-room penthouse, of course, has a large kitchen with *two* windows and enough floor space for a kitchen table and chairs. But her two bathrooms are as small as mine, and there's no window in either.

MARCH

Are you all out working in the garden? I assume March is sprouting time over there, when new shoots spring up overnight. It's a different kind of sprouting time in New York. Within three blocks of me, two fabulous new shoots have sprung up overnight, each twenty-five stories high. I will tell you how this happens.

It starts on a summer day when you're walking along Third Avenue and you pass a block-long empty lot. You walk on over to Second Avenue and pass another empty lot. A week later, there's a high construction wall around each lot. But each wall has a hole in it large enough for two human eyes. New Yorkers think it's their God-given right to supervise construction, and any builder who didn't order a hole cut in the wall would find holes cut in it for him by volunteers. So you look through the hole in each wall, and watch derricks and bulldozers turn empty lots into deep craters, and maybe you see scaffolding go up.

But by fall, there's a wooden tunnel on the sidewalk at each site, from the construction wall clear to the gutter. Its roof and sides protect you from flying debris but you can no longer look through the hole-in-the-wall. You get used to these tunnels, however, and in winter you welcome them: they keep you out of the sleeting rain and off the icy sidewalks. By which time, of course, you've forgotten why they're there. Comes a sunny day in March when you cross Third Avenue and walk over to Second and lo and behold, the tunnels are gone, the walls are gone, and two skyscraper apartment houses have shot up overnight. At the Second Avenue building you join the citizens on the sidewalk, staring critically up at the architecture and debating whether anybody wants to sit on a terrace balcony overlooking the Second Avenue truck traffic, and are they going to put shrubs and flower beds in that muddy expanse soon to be the ground floor façade? Or are they going to put a row of stores there, and if so, what kind?

We're still in suspense about the Second Avenue ground floor. But over on Third, a block-long line of plate glass store windows have been installed. On the white stone border above them, delicate pink lettering announces the coming of a flossy, six-part emporium that will offer—and I quote— Smokeworks, Gift Baskets, Bakeries, Take-Away Platters and Appetizers, a Cafe and a Charcuterie. Not living a gourmet life, I looked up charcuterie in my French dictionary, and in France it means a butcher shop. On Third Avenue I imagine it'll mean a cross between your Carvery and our Deli. Between the charcuterie and the Smokeworks—whatever they are—we're all panting to go to the Grand Opening.

The other New York harbinger of spring is the beginning of the Fifth Avenue ethnic parade season. The St. Patrick's Day parade on March 17th is the city's oldest ethnic parade and still the most popular. You put on a green sweater and join the mob lining Fifth Avenue to watch New York's sons and daughters of Erin march to the accompaniment of a dozen bands and floats. Along with Irish veterans of American wars, and paunchy gents from Irish social clubs, the marchers include hundreds of kids from Catholic schools who, whether it's snowing or ten below zero, march in green T-shirts and white shorts, from 86th Street clear down to St. Patrick's Cathedral at 50th, where the reviewing stand is. Along with the cardinal, the dignitaries on the reviewing stand always include the governor, the mayor, both senators, and assorted local congressmen and congresswomen—all wearing green bow ties or, at the very least, green carnations.

All of New York is green on St. Patrick's Day. The bakeries feature shamrock cookies, and cakes with green icing; Woolworth's has green paper hats and party decorations, and D'Agostino's supermarket runs out of pistachio ice cream.

As I said, St. Patrick's Day is the harbinger of the ethnic parades that will bloom along Fifth Avenue in the months ahead, and I intend to go into this subject in depth—including the ethnic side festivities in Central Park—when the parade season heats up this summer. Right now, I have to go buy a paperweight.

On the first warm March day I fling up the window next to my typewriter table. I did this last March when I was writing a magazine article, and one morning just as I finished retyping page nine, a March breeze suddenly blew page ten out the window and down to the sidewalk. I had to race out of the flat, ride down to the lobby and chase it a block and a half up Second Avenue to the open-air vegetable market before I finally ran down page ten halfway under the spinach bin. This March, I've got a new book in the typewriter and I don't want any trouble.

APRIL

Okay, first some unfinished business. You remember I said we'd go to the Grand Opening of that fancy emporium on Third Avenue? With the six gourmet shops? Well, there wasn't any Grand Opening. One morning, two of the shops just discreetly opened for business. The fish store was featuring hand-dipped deviled shrimp. One deviled shrimp cost a dollar seventy-five. Eighty-seven pence. If it were dipped in uranium I wouldn't pay a dollar seventy-five for one shrimp. A man in my building told me the other shop was selling a demitasse spoonful of caviar on a cracker for a dollar eighty-five. Ninety-two pence. Unbelievable.

Easter Sunday was cold and rainy here, so we didn't go to the Easter Parade, which is a fashion parade down midtown Fifth Avenue in which female New Yorkers show off their new Easter suits and bonnets. Cars are banned, and the strollers in their Easter finery take up the entire avenue as well as the sidewalks. This year the ladies shivered, and they and their escorts got rained on. But the TV cameras and fashion writers were out, and what's a little pneumonia compared with having your Easter hat on television?

It seems strange, now that spring is here, for Richard and Nina and me not to be sitting out on the front step in the evening, with Richard's Old English sheepdog, Chester, and Nina's German shepherd, Duke, my true love.

Our front step is actually a low stone ledge, enclosing the

shrubbery next to the front door, and the tenants use it in three daily shifts. The morning shift is for the baby coach brigade. When it's too April showery or muddy for Central Park, the building's young mothers sit out on the step with their coaches and strollers and infants and toddlers. Afternoons are for the retired set. Elderly convalescents sit out in deck chairs or wheelchairs with their paid "companions," taking the sun, and their retired neighbors sit on the step to chat with them. But late in the evening at ten-thirty or eleven, the early evening dating couples are replaced on the step by the late-night dog-owning brigade.

Richard and Nina and the other dog owners would sit along the step and supervise the canine Happy Hour on the sidewalk, where the dogs congregated, off leash. And every night, little dogs and big ones who lived up on the block or around the corner would come tearing down the street, dragging their owners to our sidewalk where the action was. There was a white Russian wolfhound named Czarina who lived across the street, and she was in such a hurry to get to our side she used to try to climb over Paul the doorman's car. She'd get her front paws on the car roof, and if somebody'd given her a hoist she'd have made it over here four seconds sooner.

The most fun we ever had on the step was a night last summer when I gave a birthday party for my friend Duke, the German shepherd. All his close friends came—Tinker, the Yorkie; Butch, the black and white terrier; Stanley, the dachshund; Malcolm and Benjamin, the West Highland brothers; Czarina, the white Russian wolfhound; and of course, the dog Nina refers to as "Dukey's cousin Chester," the sheepdog. I bought birthday party hats with rubber bands under the chin, and every dog wore his or her hat with solemn importance. Eric's delicatessen across the street catered the party. The birthday cake was a roast chicken, with candles stuck behind the legs and wings. Heinz, who owns the deli, put the chicken on a platter and surrounded it with chunk ends of roast beef, which he donated. We lit the candles, and I carried the lighted chicken across the street to our side. And the dogs were so awed by that platter, and by the fact that it was a party, that nobody jumped up, every dog waited for his mother to put his piece of chicken and end of roast beef on a paper birthday plate, and nobody tried to eat anybody else's. It was remarkable.

Country people in New England had a saying, of anyone who was old and got sick after Christmas. "He won't winter," they'd say. Well, Chester the sheepdog and Duke the shepherd were both old dogs, and they didn't winter. We watched Chester failing for a month before he died, early in February. But Duke was handsome and healthy then. Suddenly, in nine days, he sickened and died, three weeks after Chester. And took a piece of my heart with him.

Well, the building is still full of sociable dogs; and I have a hunch we'll be back on the step one summer night—because Richard is getting another Old English sheepdog. I'll let you know what he's like when he gets here. He hasn't been born yet; but his mother's pregnant.

MAY

Once upon a time in Central Park, there was a garden. It was perched on a small hilltop and reached by high stone steps. It had flower beds blooming in spring, summer and autumn, and a famous mulberry tree; it had a little stone moat for irrigation, with a small footbridge across it; and it was called The Shakespeare Garden. The first park gardener I met there told me it was begun in the 1900s and was modeled on Shakespeare's garden in Stratford. A later gardener said that the garden contained every flower mentioned in Shakespeare's plays. He used to identify them, for ignoramuses like me. And he always pointed out the big mulberry tree grown from a cutting of a tree in Shakespeare's own garden.

And then, six or seven years ago, the city began to fail financially, and all luxury items were cut from the budget. Among the first to go were the park gardeners. A year later, when I went up to the garden on a summer day, I found only weeds and dead flower beds. Two years after that, the old footbridge had crumbled into the empty moat, the hilltop was covered with ragged undergrowth, it was as if the garden had never been. From then on, I avoided the spot.

But a young couple who lived near the park couldn't avoid it. They walked past the abandoned hilltop on their way to work on pleasant mornings. And so, one Sunday in May a couple of years ago, Peggy-the-schoolteacher and John-the-lawyer climbed the stone steps—with buckets of earth and buckets of water and garden tools—and began to dig. They worked all day; and the next Saturday they went back to the hilltop and worked all weekend.

A few neighbors and passersby saw them working and joined them. From then on, the volunteers worked weekends all spring and summer, and all the next spring and summer. And this year the garden is beginning to bloom again.

It's not the Shakespeare Garden it once was. Peggy told me we can't get English wildflower seeds over here. So the garden has no cowslips or harebells, and there's no border of English roses anymore. But we still call it the Shakespeare Garden. And in a city of cliff dwellers, it's a small miracle to have Central Park's only garden growing again, even if it's not the English garden I loved.

Would you believe it was 94 degrees here last week? In my building we all did our closets and of course it was a mistake;

it always is. I live in a one-room flat with a small alcove. I have one large double-door closet, and an alcove linen closet with a half rack for clothes, and that's it. Everything I own has to go in those two closets, including two cartons of Christmas tree ornaments. So, like most New Yorkers, every fall I pack my summer wardrobe away in a suitcase because there's no place else to put it. Well, what happens is, there's a hot spell in spring and you naturally take the suitcase down from the shelf and unpack it and iron everything. But you can't hang your summer clothes in the closet till you've got your winter suits, dresses, pants and coats out of the closet. So you pile your winter wardrobe in your shopping-cart and wheel it up the street to the dry cleaner's to be put in box storage for the summer. And you agree to give the cleaner two weeks' notice when you want it all back. And of course, the day *after* you put everything in box storage, the temperature drops thirty degrees.

My friend Patsy Gibbs is the only New Yorker I know with enough closet space. She lives in an eight- or nine-room apartment in an old West Side family building—as distinct from newer East Side buildings like ours, which are mainly for singles and couples. Over there, they have a different problem this time of year.

"In our building," said Patsy, "the end of May is when you never can get the elevator. All the kids come home from college for the summer with their shearling coats, their bikes, boots, skis, and backpacks; their stereo sets and tape decks; their houseplants, which all look healthier and better cared-for than yours; and each kid ties up both elevators for two hours."

My friend Nina, hearing this, added gloomily:

"And the average age in this town suddenly drops a decade, and you go around all summer feeling old."

The real reason for this is that in June, hordes of new

college graduates swarm into New York from all over, to spend the summer lining up jobs. As soon as they've found jobs, they go hunting for roommates. And in September—in twos and threes—they'll start moving into *our* building and tying up *our* elevators for two hours. New York's new seeding and planting cycle.

JUNE

Fifty years ago, ground was broken for the complex of buildings originally called Radio City, now known as Rockefeller Center; and I'm going to tell you the tale of its most famous building, which opened in 1932 as the world's largest, super-colossal movie palace—Radio City Music Hall.

It seated 6,000 people on five enormous tiers, its movies were preceded by elaborate stage shows, and it boasted the world's largest pipe organ with 4,000 pipes, weighing five tons. The building's plans had been drawn up in 1929, when an organist was required to play appropriate music for the silent films in which Mary Pickford was thrown out into the snow or Lillian Gish had her virtue threatened. By the time the theatre opened, the talkies had arrived—and there was the management, with its five-ton pipe organ.

Nothing daunted, Radio City Music Hall opened every stage show with organ selections, the organ and organist bathed in a lavender spotlight. The stage show itself featured acrobats, tenors and tableaux, and its climax was the high-kicking precision dancing of a line of girls called The Rockettes. They were accompanied by a hundred-piece orchestra which rose up from the basement on a moving platform and sank back down again when the movie started. This was Radio City Music Hall, New York's prime tourist attraction through the thirties, forties and fifties.

New Yorkers themselves, of course, never went near the place unless they had children to entertain. It was so overpoweringly overdone—from its huge lobby and vast plush lounges to its ceiling murals and chandeliers—that it was a private New York joke, as I think the Alexandra Palace was to Londoners. But it had been built for tourists, and for three decades, whenever you passed the Music Hall, there were long lines of tourists waiting to get in, all year round.

But in the 1960s television replaced the movies as the most popular family entertainment and the Music Hall began to lose its appeal. By the seventies, even the children had become too sophisticated for its old-fashioned stage shows and innocuous family films, and the once-opulent palace grew shabby and down-at-heel, its murals faded, the gilt peeling off its ornate mirrors, the lounges threadbare. By 1977, the Rockettes were performing to an average audience of 300 spectators and 5,700 empty seats. And so, the management announced that it would close Radio City Music Hall and demolish the building.

New York read this news over breakfast, on the front page of *The New York Times*, and you never heard such an uproar. New Yorkers who hadn't set foot in the place since their tenth birthday wrote irate letters to *The Times*, elder statesmen and business tycoons went on TV news shows, all demanding that the city Save Radio City Music Hall. It was a landmark, it was a tradition, it was New York! The furor grew, till the Music Hall management backed down in confusion and said it would Rethink the problem. Last year, the Music Hall was sold, and it closed quietly for repairs.

It reopened two weeks ago, its murals and chandeliers restored, its palatial staircases recarpeted, its lobby and lounges gorgeously refurnished. All that's missing is the movies. Its theatre features live musical extravaganzas. The current one is a two-hour spectacular called *A New York Summer*, with

twenty-six production numbers, thirty-six high-kicking Rockettes, one thousand costumes, sixty sets, and the 200,000 moving parts of the rebuilt, five-ton pipe organ in the hands of two
eager young organists. And on Opening Night, everybody who
was anybody in New York—financiers, corporation heads,
Broadway stars, dress designers—fought to get into Radio City
Music Hall. In full evening dress.

P.S. None of them will ever set foot in it again. It's for
tourists. New Yorkers just got it back for them.

JULY

We have a new Fourth of July tradition here. Ever since
"Operation Sail," the international fleet of sailing ships
that gathered in New York harbor to celebrate our Bicenten-
nial in 1976, New Yorkers have taken to spending July
Fourth—American Independence Day—down in Lower
Manhattan.

You take the subway down to the bottom tip of the island,
where the East River and the Hudson (the west river) almost
meet at the Bay. You tour the ships that have Open House,
and you stand in Battery Park to watch the boat races and
water-skiing races. And then you walk up through the City
Hall and law courts district, and the Wall Street financial
district, buying lunch along the way at sidewalk ethnic food
booths—Greek souvlaki and strings of hot Italian sausage and
Chinese spareribs. Or you go for shrimp and clams to Sloppy
Looie's, spelled L-o-o-i-e. Best of all, in Lower Manhattan, you
just walk and gawk. It's something to gawk at.

The streets date back to the 1640s, when Lower Manhattan
was the city of New Amsterdam, capital of the Dutch colony
of New Netherlands. But along those narrow, winding, cob-
bled streets are rows of skyscrapers—hundreds of towers of

concrete and steel and glass, jutting thirty and sixty and a hundred and ten stories in the air. And they turn the winding alleys into toy canyons.

I will tell you how New Amsterdam became New York. After the Restoration in England, King Charles II looked across the water and couldn't stand the sight of a Dutch colony sitting in the middle of England's American empire. So in 1664 he sent his brother over here to take care of it. The Duke of York and his navy invaded and conquered New Netherlands. And not content with renaming the entire province of New Netherlands New York province, after himself, he also renamed the city of New Amsterdam New York City, after himself—causing no end of confusion among twentieth century Europeans who don't comprehend that New York State and New York City are not one and the same. So it served him right that when he became James II, you ran him out of England in your own Glorious Revolution. And that's enough Lower Manhattan and history.

We have a new tradition uptown this year, too. It used to be, when you walked down Fifth Avenue on a summer day, you passed old men with pushcarts selling ice cream. Well, this year, the young health food generation has taken over. One young man presides over trays of shelled walnuts, hazelnuts, cashews and so forth, to make you thirsty enough for the tables piled high with oranges, where other young men squeeze fresh orange juice for you. At a price. And down in front of St. Patrick's Cathedral, a young couple cubes iced watermelon and honeydew, and piles the melon cubes into paper cups. Try passing *them* on a hot July afternoon.

In our building, my friend Nina gave a birthday dinner for our mutual friend Richard a few weeks ago. I remember telling you once that almost nobody in New York has a garden. And the reason why I said almost nobody is that here and there, in a Manhattan highrise apartment house, there's a remarkable exception like Nina.

33

Nina lives in a penthouse on the 16th floor, and the living room double doors open onto a narrow cement terrace, twenty feet long but only five feet wide. In window boxes along the twenty-foot railing, and in pots on shelves along the opposite brick wall—sixteen floors above the street—is Nina's garden. The night of Richard's birthday dinner, we had cocktails on the terrace and I made Nina give me the names of everything growing there, so you'd know what can be done with a narrow cement terrace and a green thumb. Blooming in Nina's garden are ageratum, miniature amaryllis, miniature dahlias, dianthus, freesia, marigolds, pansies, petunias, phlox, portulacas, snapdragons, ranunculus and rose-live-forever. On a small table is an orange tree, with baby oranges popping out all over. And at opposite ends of the terrace are two dwarf apple trees, one of them covered with blossoms. (The other one's ailing.)

Nina owned Duke, my true love, the German shepherd who died last winter; and she used to get very wrathful when he ate her flowers. I'd ring the bell to take him to the park, and Nina'd open the door and say: "Your boyfriend had a little African violet salad for breakfast; I'm not speaking to him."

But at Richard's party, when somebody admired the deep purple pansies, Nina touched one of the pansy faces and said:

"Duke used to love to eat the pansies. He'd never eat a whole one, you know; he'd just nibble a petal here and there so I wouldn't notice. It doesn't seem right, to come out here and not find a few petals nibbled off."

AUGUST

In a book I wrote about New York, I remarked that New

Yorkers in summer divide into two groups: those who always go away weekends, and those who never go away weekends. I'm in the never-go-away-weekends class. I refuse to pack, take a bus to the station, take a train to Long Island, unpack, and then have to do the whole thing over again, a day and a half later.

Nina is not a weekender either, but Richard loves weekending, and mostly can't get away. He's an executive. He runs a big computer operation, he walks around wearing a beeper seven days a week, he keeps it by his bed at night, and when the beeper goes off, it means Call Your Office, there's an emergency. Very impressive. And he has a fancy, air-conditioned car, and when he can't get away for a whole weekend, he wants to drive us all to Jones Beach on Sunday—his buddy, Schor, and Nina and me.

He has this system for beating the traffic and the beach crowds. He leaves here at seven a.m. when there's no traffic, arriving at Jones Beach at nine a.m. when it's deserted. By one, when the beach is crowded, he's had enough sun and he drives home against the traffic. But I crawl out of bed at seven a.m. six days a week and I like to sleep late on Sunday; and I'd rather spend the day touring Central Park than frying on a beach. So every time Richard invites me, I decline.

Well, last Sunday Richard and Schor left for Jones Beach at seven a.m. and got there at nine, when the town was asleep and the beach deserted. Richard got himself nicely slathered with suntan oil and stretched out and closed his eyes. And his beeper went off. Call Your Office. It took them twenty minutes to find a phone, and five minutes after that, they were driving back to town, because one of Richard's computers had broken down and the Sunday man didn't know how to fix it.

So as I said, you're better off in Central Park. You go over about one, with a couple of sections of the Sunday *Times*, and spend the day in a rowboat or under a tree. And you take a picnic supper, because summer park evenings are marvelous.

On the Sheep Meadow, there may be a concert by the Philharmonic, or a Puccini opera by the Met. The Sheep Meadow—five blocks long and several blocks wide—is endless acres of grass, and you keep squeezing closer together on the grass till the meadow seats 250,000 people. The concerts and operas are free; so are the nightly performances at the Shakespeare Theatre in Central Park. But the theatre only seats three thousand, so you get on line early in the afternoon because the tickets are given out at six and they're gone in half an hour. You sit on line on the grass and after you get your ticket, you eat your picnic supper on the grass.

My friend Didi, who lived next door to me in 8-F, did things differently. Didi was very pretty and very feminine, and she loved the flossy Victorian graces. She used to invite a host of friends to a picnic-before-Shakespeare-in-the-park; they'd meet at her place, and when they left for the picnic, I'd see them parade down the hall, one young man carrying a covered silver platter, another carrying the wine bucket, the girls with Didi's best salad bowls in their arms, and Didi herself bringing up the rear with a wicker basket of silver flatware, linen cloth and linen napkins. You had to see it to believe it, when she spread all this out on the grass in Central Park and started serving everything graciously—before the fascinated gaze of three thousand pickle-and-hot-dog-eating peasants.

Walking home from the park at ten last Sunday night, when Schor and I came to Park Avenue we knew it was summer. Park Avenue is still where the very rich live, and of course they close the apartment-in-town and go away for the summer. Crossing Park Avenue, we saw rows of tall apartment houses, absolutely black. Schor pointed up to a single light in one dark building and said:

"The super's home!"

At Third Avenue and Second, where the wage earners live, every building was lit up. Most people were back from their weekends by then. But not all. What we stay-at-homes *love* to do on a summer Sunday night is sit out late on our front step and watch the cabs drive up with the last homecoming weekenders.

They crawl out of the cab, hot, tired, sunburnt, rumpled from the train ride, lugging suitcases and tennis rackets and golf clubs. And as they stumble bleary-eyed and exhausted toward the front door, one of us will say brightly:

"Didja have a good time?"

They just grunt.

SEPTEMBER

The story I'm going to tell you happened a few years ago, on a September Saturday night still known on our block as The Night of the White Poodle.

He was a very large poodle, he lived across the street with his owner, a young artist, on the second floor of a five-story brownstone, and he loved to stand at the broad, high picture window and watch the world go by below.

At ten-thirty on a September Saturday night, Nina, Richard and I were sitting on the front step with the dogs, when we noticed that the poodle, standing in the picture window, had got his leg caught in a drapery cord and was struggling to free it. The living room light had been left on for the poodle; the artist was obviously not home. The upper floors of the brownstone were dark.

As we watched the poodle struggle, Heinz ran out of Eric's Delicatessen next door to the brownstone and up the high front steps of the poodle's building. On the top step he was level with the bottom of the picture window. But below the window was a sheer, two-story drop to Ruc's, a Czech restaurant in the basement. Risking his neck, Heinz leaned far out across the abyss, feeling for a latch along the base of the window.

People had come up out of the restaurant meanwhile, and were looking up at Heinz and the poodle. Heinz came back down and told the crowd the window had no latch. But he would phone the artist's answering service; they might know where to reach him. Heinz went back into the deli, but the crowd stayed on, watching the poodle anxiously.

Ten minutes later, Bill—owner of Rooney's Liquor Store next to the deli—came out and ran up the poodle's front steps, opened the front door and disappeared inside. When he came out, he told the crowd he'd rung all the doorbells but no tenants were home.

By this time, in the apartment houses on our side of the street, concerned citizens were leaning out of sixth- and tenth- and fifteenth-story windows, watching the poodle, and it may have been one of them who called the police. At eleven-twenty, a squad car arrived, and two burly cops jumped out, ran up the steps of the poodle's house and disappeared inside. Ruc's restaurant and the movie theatre up the block were both emptying out by then, and their patrons swelled the crowd under the poodle's window. And a large contingent of late-night dog walkers had collected on our side of the street, all now waiting expectantly for the police to rescue the poodle. But the cops came out and said that the inside front door was locked and they had no legal authority to force the lock since no crime was being committed. They climbed back into the squad car and drove off.

I don't know who called the Fire Department. At eleven-forty-five, a fire truck careened round the corner and stopped at the poodle's house, and two firemen jumped down and ran a ladder up to the poodle's window. One fireman went up the ladder and examined the window frame. Then he came down and told the crowd that there was no way to remove the window and he had no legal authority to smash it since there wasn't any fire. The firemen got back in the truck and drove off.

Now all this time the poodle, struggling vainly to free his leg, had to stop now and then to rest. And when he did, he was very interested in everything that was going on. He was especially interested in the firemen's ladder and the crowds under his window and the increasing number of heads leaning out of windows on our side of the street. Though he didn't know the cause, the poodle could tell this was a very big night.

At twelve-oh-five a.m., the poodle suddenly got his leg free. A cheer went up as he trotted off out of sight; and the crowd melted away. Only a few of us were left, talking it over on the front step, when a few minutes later the poodle came back to the window.

"He probably just wanted a drink of water," said Nina. "Look at him; he's wondering where everybody went."

On Sunday, we heard that the artist had come home at three a.m., phoned his answering service and gotten five messages:

Call Eric's Delicatessen.

Call Rooney's Liquor Store.

Call Ruc's Restaurant.

Call the 67th Police Precinct house.

Call the 76th Street Fire Station.

By Sunday afternoon, the drapes were down.

NINETEEN EIGHTY

1980

MARCH

I hope you don't mind if I talk about radio? I'm about to turn
English music lovers green with envy because the New York
area has ten radio stations which play classical music. Seven of
them play other kinds of music, too; they're owned by
colleges, and run by students. But the remaining three
stations play only classical music, twenty-four hours a day, so
an insomniac can listen to Bach and Beethoven all night long.
One of the three is owned by the City of New York. The other
two are commercially owned and bombard you with ads,
including one pair of ads that drives me up the wall.

You're listening to a symphony one evening, and when it
ends, there's a pause and a portentous male voice announces:

"You are invited to spend an evening with Civilization."
Now if you're sitting in a New York apartment listening to a
radio, it's hard to see how you could spend an evening *without*
civilization. And if you hear this ad once, you hear it six times
a day, seven days a week, for six months. Then the advertiser
changes the message. Once more, when the concert you're
listening to ends, the same pontifical voice informs you:

"There are moments which are larger and grander than
Life."

No, there aren't. But you'll listen to that idiotic statement for six months, too. What both these ads are in aid of is the Metropolitan Opera Company, which wants to sell you a ticket. The Met is a very great opera company where you can hear opera magnificently sung, but you won't have the slightest idea what the singers are singing about since the only language the Met declines to sing opera in is English. So at the Met, Queen Mary Stuart is *Maria* Stuarda, Rob Devereux, beloved of Elizabeth the First, is *Roberto*, and Scott's Bride of Lammermoor isn't plain Lucy, she's *Lucia*. If in spite of this, you want to buy a Met subscription, go right ahead. A single orchestra seat to seven operas won't cost you more than three hundred dollars, or twenty-three pounds per opera.

Enough of that. I wish to congratulate my friends Laird and Reid White, who after sixteen years of marriage recently celebrated their fourth wedding anniversary. They were married in 1964—on February 29. Laird was one of two pretty girls who lived next door to me at the time. We met through a present Reid gave her while he was courting her.

I live on the eighth floor and I work by the window in an alcove off the living room. Jutting out at a right angle from my alcove window is the living room window of the flat next door; and one fall morning in '63, I looked up from my typewriter to see a fat grey cat lying on the next-door windowsill staring at me. When our eyes met, he waved his tail. I don't like cats, but you have to be neighborly. I waved back. After that, we waved at each other several times a day. Now and then I asked him how he was.

And then one evening, I came out of the kitchen to find the cat standing on my telephone table by the alcove window. My front door was closed. The cat had jumped from his open window in through mine across a sheer, eight-story drop to the street below.

"You could've got killed!" I told him. He cooed.

I picked him up and carried him next door to 8-F and rang the bell. Didi opened the door and I said:

"Your cat just jumped through my window."

"He is not my cat," said Didi firmly. "Laird!" she called. "Come get your miserable cat, he flew in 8-G's window."

Laird, another pretty blonde, came and collected the cat and told me he was a present from her boyfriend and that his name was Clawed—C-l-a-w-e-d—because that's what he did to everybody. And she kept their side living room window closed thereafter.

MAY

A hundred thousand New Yorkers ought to send thank-you notes to former Mayor John Lindsay. He's just changed their lives. Back in 1966, Lindsay was inaugurated on a freezing January day at the beginning of a transit strike. For two icy weeks, with no buses or subways running, people who lived several miles from their offices couldn't get to work. Lindsay gave the strikers their pay increase, but he won a concession in return. Thereafter, their contracts would expire not on January first, but on April first.

Well, this year—on April first—the transit workers struck again. But this time it was spring. The joggers began jogging to work; other New Yorkers began biking and roller-skating to work; and people who'd never walked further than the nearest bus stop discovered they had feet and began walking to work. Some of them went along the major avenues. But for the next two weeks—early in the morning and late in the afternoon—the eight hundred and forty acres of Central Park were sprinkled with joggers, bikers, skaters and walkers who were just in time to goggle at the sea of white apple blossoms, followed by the flowering of the white cherry trees. The strike was over by the time the lilac and the Japanese pink cherry were in bloom, but the bikers, skaters and walkers were still in the park to see them. Since the day the strike ended—and though the fare hasn't risen yet—the number of riders on New York buses and subways has dropped by one hundred thousand a day.

The dogs are also out in force, enjoying the spring. You see them going into the cleaner's, the hardware store, the deli— but mostly you see them tied by their leashes to the parking meters at curbs in front of supermarkets. Some dogs enjoy being tied there, to watch the passing parade. Some dogs do not.

Take the dachshund who's been out walking with his mother and the baby. He notices that while his mother left him and the baby's carriage outside the supermarket, she took the baby in with her. The dachshund suspects he's been something of a nuisance to her since the baby came, and he wouldn't put it past her to sneak out a back door with the baby and move to Pittsburgh. So he sends up a shrill, angry barking, the gist of which is: "I know you're in there!"

Then there's the Irish setter owned by a young couple. He has complete faith in their constancy and no faith at all in their ability to remember where they left him. So he barks— loudly and anxiously—to remind them that they brought him, and to provide them with his exact location. It is the acid test of a writer's love of dogs, to be typing by her open window, with the dachshund and the Irish setter barking side by side, at parking meters directly below the window.

New York breaks out in a rash of block parties in spring and summer. One block will bake things and make things to raise money to plant trees on the block. A long avenue will hold a party to call attention to its neighborhood stores. I'll describe one of them for you sometime. But I never pass a block party without remembering the spring when our Democratic Club got carried away and decided to hold its annual fund-raising dinner-dance on a city street, like a block party. Oh, there were a few Cassandras who warned that something would go wrong, we'd forget something essential, but we paid no heed to them.

In true block-party fashion, we got a permit from City Hall to use a side street—lined with brownstone walk-ups—and a permit from the Police Department to close the street to traffic. We ordered elegant box dinners from a fancy restaurant; and on the great day we set up rented tables along both sidewalks, we put candles and flowers on every table, and set a record player out in the middle of the street to play music for dancing. And at seven o'clock of a May Saturday evening we assembled, two hundred strong, the women in long gowns, the men—including judges, congressmen, city councilmen—in full dinner dress.

All went swimmingly, until coffee was served. It was then that a gentleman rose, sought out a member of the Dinner Committee, leaned down and asked her a confidential question. At the question, her face froze in horror. When she finally answered, the gentleman's face froze in complete panic. The word the gentleman used was "john," but I'll translate it for you. The question he asked was: "Where's the loo?" The answer he got was: "There isn't any."

For the rest of the long, long evening, dignified judges and learned counsels, in their formal evening clothes, could be seen haggling with the janitors of brownstone rooming houses, to whom they paid steadily rising prices for the use of ancient, unsanitary loos in the basements of brownstone tenements.

If the gentlemen had been in any condition to walk three long crosstown blocks, I could've made a fortune renting out my bathroom.

JUNE

This has been Crazy Spring in New York—crazy weather and
crazy people both. To begin with, May ended with a mid-
summer heat wave six weeks early, and during the heat wave
several thousand New York bike riders took part in a mara-
thon, pedaling round and round Central Park for twenty-
four straight hours, half the hours under a ninety-degree sun.
The winner of this insanity was a young man who biked four
hundred and forty-five miles in twenty-four hours. WHY,
nobody said.

To continue, June arrived hot and sunny, so of course we
all took our wool clothes to the cleaner's to be put in box
storage. Then we came home, took our summer wardrobes
out of their suitcases, washed and ironed them and hung
them in the closet, whereupon the temperature dropped to
forty-seven degrees in the city, and there was snow upstate, in
a June cold wave that broke all weather department records.

So by last week, even my neighborhood began to look crazy
to me. I live three blocks from the East River, but I rarely walk
east; somehow all my normal destinations are north, west and
south of me. So when I walked east with a friend last week, I
got my first look at some fairly new neighborhood sights.

One, on 73rd Street, is a long low building with a dome
rising behind it. Inside, the dome becomes a thirty-two-foot-
high inverted bowl ceiling, entirely covered in pleated white
fabric. What it's the ceiling of is our local gym, where you can
take classes in tumbling, pole vaulting, rythmic gymnastics
and dancing. Women of my acquaintance trudge there early
in the morning to exercise classes, on their way to offices
where they sit-and-spread all day. What any New Yorker
wants with pole vaulting lessons, I couldn't tell you.

Then there's the Plant Supermarket, where you can buy an
enormous variety of plants, flowers, seeds, everything you

need for your vegetable garden, and a wide assortment of trees including apple, orange and cherry. And there's nothing crazy about this rural supermarket except that it runs from 73rd Street through to 72nd, smack in the middle of sky-scraper Manhattan.

Next door to the plant market is the Kennelworth, spelled K-e-n-n-e-l-worth and billed as New York's Luxury Hotel for Pets. Millionaire dogs are left there while their families vacation in Europe. Since my own canine friends are all middle-class dogs, I can't tell you what the luxury hotel looks like inside.

And honesty compels me to admit that the lovely sight around the corner from me is probably just as crazy. People who've lived in this neighborhood for years have walked past it hundreds of times and still don't know it's there. On 71st Street, there's a row of brownstone houses with stores at street level. Between two of these stores is an alleyway so narrow most people walk past it without seeing it. And I don't remember when, or why, I first turned into it, but if you walk a few steps into the alleyway, you find yourself in a perfect English mews. Nobody seems to know how it got there or who lives in it. A few of us have taken visitors there for years, and we've never seen a soul come out of, or go into, one of the small mews houses. But every spring we find them freshly painted, and the flower boxes outside the curtained windows freshly filled.

And finally, there's a more distant, and much newer, neighborhood sight, which compresses the history of these crazy times. On a block in the mid-sixties there's a row of millionaire town houses. One of them has been bombed twice, but it's the only one of three houses that caused a woman on the block to tell a TV newsman she thought the block ought to have permanent police protection. The house that was bombed twice belongs to the PLO. The second of the three houses belongs to David Rockefeller, who many New Yorkers think was chiefly responsible for bringing the Shah of Iran to New York last November. The third house was recently bought, and is now occupied, by Richard Nixon. I don't walk down that block myself.

I close with a happier item, thanks to you. A year ago, I told you about the Shakespeare Garden in Central Park which had gone to seed when the city could no longer afford gardeners, and which a handful of New Yorkers had begun to recreate. I said that the new garden could never be a real Shakespeare garden, since we couldn't get English wildflower seeds over here. Well, a few generous Woman's Hour listeners promptly rushed out and mailed us wildflower seeds, and I am now able to report that the cowslips and harebells are blooming, and so is the dyer's wort. And along the rustic wooden fence at the far rim of the garden—for the first time in ten years—the gold-centered, white English garden roses are blooming again. The Shakespeare Gardeners thank you, New York thanks you, and I can't tell you what it meant to me, to see the long row of yellow buds flower into white roses again, like a line of small Phoenixes rising from the ashes. Thank you!

JULY

We've had a food revolution over here. We used to be resigned to supermarket fruits and vegetables—pale carrots wrapped in tinted plastic to make them look bright orange; sour berries in tightly wrapped boxes; and when you needed a couple of onions you had to buy a bag of twelve. Well, a few years ago, Korean and Vietnamese immigrants began opening fresh fruit and vegetable markets, and now they're all over town, in hole-in-the-wall storefronts with extra stalls out on the sidewalk. You pick out the brightest bunch of unwrapped carrots, and two or three best onions, and you can taste a berry before you buy a box.

And in summer there's something new called Greenmarkets. Every Saturday, New Jersey farmers come to town and set up stalls wherever the city has space for them. Our neighborhood's Greenmarket is in a schoolyard at 67th Street and First Avenue, and on Saturday mornings Nina and I walk down to buy fresh Jersey tomatoes, peaches and corn on the cob, comparison shopping at four or five stalls, each presided over by a farmer and his family.

And for dessert, there are the cookie carts on Fifth Avenue. Cookies—you call them biscuits—used to be had only in mass-produced supermarket boxes or at expensive bakeries. But last spring, a few enterprising young New Yorkers—male and female both—began to bake big, old-fashioned cookies, oatmeal and molasses and chocolate chip, and sell them at carts up and down the avenue. The chocolate chip cookies became so popular, and the rival carts so competitive, that *New York* magazine ran a long, solemn article headed "The Chocolate Chip Cookie War." All I can say is, you'll never run into a sweeter war.

My next item will annoy any bird-watchers listening. Sorry about that. Dog Hill in Central Park is a broad, sloping hill several city blocks long, where city dogs (illegally) run free. On spring weekend afternoons, it's a vast canine cocktail party. But on summer weekdays, the hill is empty until five p.m. when the worst of the sun's heat is gone. Then a few regulars arrive: two golden retrievers, a placid white spitz, a very sociable brown Doberman, and a black toy poodle who barks a lot, to make up for the fact that he's little.

Well, at that hour, the thicket of trees at the crest of the hill is loud with the singing of more birds than I know the names of. And on the ground, robins and wrens hop about, pecking like chickens at whatever food they find in the grass, paying no attention at all to the large dogs bounding after a ball nearby, or to the small poodle's barking. When the dogs have a race, the birds just flutter up a few feet in the air to let the race go by, and then settle back down in the grass and go on pecking, and the birds in the trees go on singing.

This baffled me, because bird-watchers had persuaded me that birds are easily frightened. All year round when I'm walking in the park, singing or kicking leaves, I am shushed by bird-watchers who tiptoe up to a tree and stand looking up without breathing, for fear of scaring the birds away. So I consulted Nina about this contradiction.

"Birds," said Nina judiciously, "don't like bird-watchers. Bird-watchers stare at them, invading their privacy, so birds hide from them. Dogs pay no attention to the birds, so the birds like them."

I gotta tell you about Nina's bumblebee. Last year, a bee came every day to pollinate her flowers. The old wooden terrace door had a hole in the top, and when the bee got tired, he crawled into the hole and took a nap. But last fall Nina had a new door installed. And the next day the bee came and worked, and then looked for his nap-hole. He searched more and more frantically for it, before he gave up and flew off. And this spring, he didn't come back. Nina was inconsolable. Her orange tree had no blossoms and there was nobody to open the snapdragons; but more than that, she missed him.

"He was a lovely bumblebee," she told me sadly. "The two of us worked out there together, we never bothered each other; we were companions."

Well, last week I was on her terrace one afternoon, and I don't know what made me ask: "Did your bumblebee ever come back?" And Nina's mouth set in a disapproving line.

"His son was here this morning," she said. "He's an adolescent, he has no manners. He kept flying in my face. And he dashed all over the place, from this flower to that, and then back to the first one. He hasn't any idea what he's doing!"

"He'll learn," I said. "One day he'll be grown up and sedate, and you'll probably be sorry."

Last year, Nina's son, Claudie was an adolescent. Now he's finished college, he's grown up and independent, he's joined the Marines and you have to call him Chuck.

AUGUST

The news media have told you what happened at the Democratic National Convention, but they never tell you what it's like to be part of our quadrennial insanity. In 1976, my friend Lolly was a delegate to the convention and she gave me an in-depth report on the festivities. That year, as this year, the Democratic convention was held in New York, at Madison Square Garden. Now Madison Square Garden is a vast indoor amphitheatre. But delegations from fifty states—plus Guam, Puerto Rico and the Virgin Islands—have to be seated in it, and they can't all sit up front.

So what happens is, the first twenty delegations can see and hear everything going on at the podium; the next twenty delegations can't see the podium but can hear most of the debates; and the last thirteen or so delegations can't see or hear anything but the loudly amplified speeches. In 1976, the New York delegation was way in the back, and Lolly never got to see the podium or hear the debates. Neither did my friend Stuart, the alternate. Every delegate has an alternate, a stand-in. But the alternates were seated upstairs in the visitors' gallery, and the New York delegation was in the back of *that*.

This is why the leader of each delegation has a microphone

and several telephones. If his delegation is in the back, he gets news of what's going on from a floor manager with a walkie-talkie and he relays this news to his delegation over the microphone. He has to shout into the mike because the delegation in front of or alongside him is having a caucus which is supposed to be a discussion, but is usually a shouting match between opposing factions in the delegation.

The telephones connect the delegates with their candidate's trailer—caravan—parked outside and more importantly, with the visitors' gallery upstairs because every time there's an important vote coming up, two delegates are in the loo and a third has gone for coffee, so you have to phone the visitors' gallery and tell three alternates to rush down to the floor and vote.

Since convention sessions begin late in the day, most delegates have a great deal of free time; and when New York is the host city, its delegates are also hosts and hostesses to the visiting delegations.

"If you're very rich," Lolly told me, "the Campaign Committee honors you by letting you entertain a large delegation for the entire week. You give them a lavish cocktail party, you get matinee tickets for them, you take them all to lunch at the best restaurants, and since they're your guests, you pay for everything. The very rich," Lolly assured me, "compete fiercely for this honor."

Lolly herself volunteered to take the entire Illinois delegation to the Statue of Liberty one morning. She hurried down to Battery Park in Lower Manhattan an hour ahead of time and bought two hundred ferry boat tickets to the statue. And at the appointed hour, instead of the two hundred delegates and alternates, four wives and three children showed up: the delegation had been summoned to an unexpected morning caucus on the subject of the Vice Presidential nominees.

Most delegates live a thousand to three thousand miles

from the host city and all delegates must pay their own expenses—air fare and hotel bills—which makes you wonder why so many thousands of men and women compete fiercely for *that* honor.

"The purpose of being a delegate," Lolly explained to me, "is to get your face on television, to impress the folks back home. You know how the delegates wander up and down the aisles all the time? They're looking for a news commentator so they can go home and say:

'Did you see me on television? I was right behind Walter Cronkite.'"

I will be very glad when summer is over and my vacationing neighbors come home. I am the eighth floor's Keeper of the Keys. I had to water the plants in 8-E while Susan was on her honeymoon; I had to let the painters into 8-H and lock up after them; and when Blossom, in 8-A, went to Egypt, she gave me a spare key in case the friend who was coming daily to feed the two cats lost her key. So naturally, when the man in the flat next to Blossom's thought he smelled gas escaping—at six o'clock on a Saturday morning—I was the one the super woke up. I staggered down the hall with him and let him into Blossom's apartment whereupon the two cats streaked out and down the hall to my place and hid in my kitchen broom closet, and it took me half an hour to find them, catch them and carry them back to their empty apartment.

Never mind. At twilight of a warm summer evening, a music-loving friend and I walk a green short cut through Central Park to Lincoln Center where we have a salad-plate supper at the outdoor cafeteria and sit over coffee watching the play of the fountains till the bell summons us inside for one of the Mostly Mozart concerts, the supper and concert together costing less than a five-pound note. On such evenings, I'm glad I was too broke to go away myself this summer.

SEPTEMBER

In honor of the fall season (autumn to you), everybody in my building is redecorating, or cleaning like crazy trying to make our shabby old furniture sparkle like new. I decided to get all the old wax off my dinette chairs and did it so enthusiastically I took most of the finish off as well. I scrubbed the kitchen cabinets taking some of the paint off, and washed my curtains, and I'm waiting for Richard to come up and hang them. As soon as he's calmed down.

Richard sent his air conditioner out to be cleaned and repaired, and took down his Venetian blind and put it in the bathtub, to hose it down under the shower. But the repair shop phoned to tell him his air conditioner was beyond repair and when he turned the shower full on the blind, the water pressure split the binding, and his Venetian blind fell apart in the bathtub.

But the surest sign that a new year is beginning is that everybody is on a self-improvement drive. From New York University at 8th Street, to Hunter College at 68th, half of New York is registering at some college for night courses in Philosophy or the History of Art which most of them will drop out of on the first sleeting winter night. And I, who hate novels, have begun lugging Joyce Carol Oates and V. S. Naipaul and Doris Lessing home from the library, in an attempt to Improve my Mind. This literary self-improvement is not special to me; it sweeps half the country over here, every fall, like an epidemic. Every big city from Boston to Chicago breaks out in a rash of book-and-author luncheons and book-and-author dinners. Tickets are sold to four or five hundred people, to a luncheon or dinner at which three or four authors will appear as guest speakers, to discuss their new books.

So if you're an author with a book coming out in the fall, your publisher's publicity department works hard to get you invited, as a speaker, to the Cleveland dinner or the Philadelphia luncheon. Your expenses are paid by the publisher who expects you to make a speech about your book, so brilliant, so witty, so enticing, that all five hundred guests will rush up to your table afterwards and buy your book, for the privilege of having you autograph it.

That table is an author's Purgatory. At every book-and-author luncheon or dinner, after the dessert, coffee and speeches, the management sets up a table for each author/speaker, at the back of the dining room. Copies of your book are stacked high on the table and you stand behind it with a bright, fixed smile on your face and pray somebody will come up and buy your book.

Well, I had a book coming out here this month, and I was one of four speakers at a book-and-author dinner in Pittsburgh, Pennsylvania. The other three were men and on these occasions, a male author simply does not know what trouble is. He puts on a clean shirt and a dark suit or he's told it's "black tie" and he's all set. A female author who knows September is too late for a summer dress and not early enough for a winter one, always has a problem. My problem was simple: I have only one elegant dinner outfit. It's a black velvet pantsuit and a white satin blouse, and the problem was I was afraid I'd look ridiculous in black velvet in September. But I phoned my high-fashion friend Arlene, since she was the original owner of the pantsuit, and she assured me that among the very *chic*, velvet is now considered a year-round fabric.

So off I went to Pittsburgh, and made my speech with confidence, knowing that in the black velvet pantsuit and the white satin blouse I looked stunning. My clothes even carried me through the ordeal of standing behind the table—and twenty Heaven-sent people came up and bought my book—so I was feeling both *chic* and successful when the evening officially came to an end.

But I walked back to the hotel with one of my fellow authors and we agreed we both needed a drink. I swept regally ahead of him into the hotel's cocktail lounge and we took a table and let our jackets fall behind us over the backs of the chairs. And it wasn't until a pretty young waitress came up to the table to take our order that I noticed the waitresses' costumes. All four of them were attractively dressed—in white satin blouses and black velvet pants.

From then on, every traveling salesman (what you call a commercial traveler) who dropped into a seat at a nearby table for a solitary nightcap, stared disapprovingly at me. Why was this aging hostess, who was obviously supposed to be overseeing the young waitresses, instead sitting at a table casually having a drink with a customer?

To end on a high note: next month, the book is coming out in London, and on October 6 I'm flying over for a week, to do some publicity for it there. If you happen to see a lady of uncertain age sashaying around town one evening in a white satin blouse and black velvet pantsuit, come up and say hello to me.

NOVEMBER

Just before I left for London in October, I got a note in the mail. "Dear Miss Hanff," it said, "My sisters in England listen to your 'Woman's Hour' broadcasts, which make them feel they know what our life is like, since you live on East 72nd Street and my wife and I live on East 74th Street. The purpose of this note is to invite you to our Block Party on Saturday." I went to the block party, but this is the first chance I've had to deliver a message to his sisters, from the gentleman who wrote the note. The message from Brother Henry on East 74th Street to his sisters Elizabeth (in St. Albans), Amelia (in Clapham), Mary (in Westminster), Victoria (in Suffolk) and Sarah (in Sussex) is that the block party was a huge success.

The block was closed to traffic for the day, and the street and sidewalks were jammed with stalls, selling T-shirts and sweaters, and jewelry and china ornaments and plants and pillows and paintings and old books, in a giant white elephant sale. But the main attraction at a block party is always the food. There was Japanese teriyaki and sizzling Italian sausages, and shish kebab, and flossy plates of paté and brie, but most popular of all were the tables where residents of the block sold their own homemade specialties. Henry wants you to know he made a double batch of sconns (we Americans firmly call them scones). A mother and daughter made Alsatian crepes with assorted fillings. And there were homemade cookies and brownies and carrot cakes and apple pies to take home for dinner. The party ended with a raffle in which practically everybody won one of the prizes donated by local merchants: a pair of movie tickets, dinner for two at the corner restaurant, a haircut and shampoo for the family dog, and so forth. Henry's American wife, Patricia, was treasurer and told me that the block party raised nearly seven thousand dollars, to be spent on trees.

Just trees? Well, first the committee will hire a contractor to uproot and cart away the block's diseased and dying old trees. Then they'll hire a nurseryman to sell them the ten new trees he thinks will grow best in small plots of earth on a city sidewalk. When the trees are planted, an expert bricklayer will be hired to build brick fences around them, high enough on the sidewalk to keep out dogs, low enough on the gutter side to provide a runoff after rain. And finally, a florist will advise which flowers will grow best at the base of each tree. So now Henry's sisters have a full report on the block party.

Tomorrow is Thanksgiving, and I'm pleased to report that my dinner guests will include a newly resident Old English sheepdog, and thereby hangs a tale. Richard, owner of Chester-the-sheepdog who died two years ago, drove out to the kennel last summer to see about getting a new pup. He ordered his pup but he saw a sight at the kennel that depressed him. A massive, full-grown Old English sheepdog was kept in a cage barely big enough for him. He'd been living in the cage for three months. The dog's name was Bentley, and for the first two years of his life he had lived with a family in Vermont. Then the family had to move to England for a year, and rather than quarantine Bentley there for six months, they decided to leave him behind. They drove him to the kennel, said to the breeder, "Find a home for him," and drove off. Bentley couldn't believe his family had abandoned him. When he was locked in the cage, he went berserk—tearing at the steel wire and barking until he was worn out. Finally, he gave up. When Richard saw him, Bentley sat in the cage hour after hour, staring at nothing, as motionless as a block of wood. Richard pitied the dog but he didn't want him. Nobody wanted him. Everybody wanted a pup.

On a Saturday afternoon in September Richard drove up to the kennel for his pup, and when he got back he phoned me.

"Did you get your pup?" I asked. "What's his name?"

There was a pause.

"Bentley," said Richard. "I warn you. He's a nerd. He just sits. But I couldn't stand leaving him in that cage." He added that Bentley had come alive enough to go over every inch of his new home with his nose, so there was hope.

"Bring him up," I said.

Richard came up a few minutes later, accompanied by the most beautiful Old English sheepdog I ever saw, with a thick snow-white coat and enormous white fur paws. I sat in my armchair, and at Richard's command Bentley sat alongside the chair with his profile to me. His face was entirely hidden under a mop of white fur, and he stared off at nothing. I leaned down and, talking into his left ear, told Bentley he was the most beautiful sheepdog in the world. I told him there were lots of dogs in the neighborhood who would be over-joyed to meet him. I told him he was going to be very happy in his new home with Richard, and that all the people who lived in the building were going to admire him and appreciate him, and all the dogs were going to be friends with him. He sat, unmoving, with no sign that he heard me. Finally I ran out of things to say and stopped talking. I looked at Richard and sighed, and Richard shrugged.

And, still staring straight ahead and without moving any-thing else, Bentley offered me his paw.

And a Happy Thanksgiving to you, too.

DECEMBER

Now that you've finished your Christmas shopping, I'll tell you what gifts you might have bought, for the friend-who-has-everything. The following items were taken from three Christmas catalogues that had to be read to be believed.

Item No. 1 is from the Gucci catalogue. It's a lizard handbag and it has an eighteen-karat-gold handle that can be detached and worn as a necklace. So Gucci probably thinks it's a bargain—at only eleven thousand five hundred dollars.

Item No. 2 comes from the catalogue of Hammacher-Schlemmer, a home-furnishings store like no other. For example, the Hammacher-Schlemmer catalogue, in these energy-shortage times, advertised not only an electric foot-warmer and an electric fish-scaler, but an electric record-cleaner for your dusty record albums. Well, their prize gift this year is for the executive in your life. It's an electronic desk fitted out with an electric cigarette lighter, an electric pencil sharpener, an electric paper shredder, a digital clock, a digital thermometer, an electric calculator, a radio, a cassette player and recorder, and a small color TV set. All this, for only eight thousand nine hundred and fifty dollars—making it cheaper than the Gucci handbag. But of course, that's not including what the desk's ten electric gadgets will do to your monthly electric bill, which would turn even Gucci pale.

And finally an item from Neiman Marcus. Neiman Marcus, a Texas emporium, famous for suggesting you buy your spouse a nice little helicopter or motor launch for Christmas, opened a multi-million-dollar store in a New York suburb. Their prize catalogue item is described as "the Earth as only the astronauts have seen it." It's a globe of the world, revolving on a special base. The globe and base together weigh four hundred and ninety-five pounds. If you can get it through your front door, and are willing to knock out a couple of walls to make space for it in your living room, you can have this globe, personally delivered and installed by an expert, for only fourteen thousand five hundred dollars.

Never mind. All this insanity is nicely balanced by the wonderful small shops in New York where you can buy offbeat gifts for only a few dollars. My favorite shop is called The Elder Craftsmen. All its items are handmade by men and women who are over the age of sixty. You can buy Christmas tree ornaments there that include a hand-carved wooden sled, a pair of felt penguins and a gnome made of a walnut shell and wearing a bright red peaked cap. You can buy a mobile of felt figures from Beatrix Potter's *Peter Rabbit*, and another with figures from *The Nutcracker*. You can buy handmade baby boots and mittens and handmade toys, including a four-foot-long stuffed cotton dachshund.

But my favorite gift this year came from *The New York Times*. It cost two dollars and fifty cents, and I'm giving it as a small extra present to my seven Christmas dinner guests. I found out the birth date—day, month and year—of each guest and mailed the list of dates to a store owned by *The Times*. And I got back a Xerox of the front page of *The New York Times* published on the day each guest was born. Each front page came neatly rolled like a diploma, to be wrapped and put at the guest's place, but suitable for framing later.

In spite of a bleak sign of inflation, Christmas in New York is as lovely as ever this year. All the big churches had their usual marvelous concerts. We went to one at St. Thomas's on Fifth Avenue called "An English Christmas," to hear English choral music from William Byrd to Benjamin Britten and to join in singing English Christmas carols. And we went to St. Bartholomew's on Park Avenue to hear the Bach *Magnificat*. But the churches, too, are feeling the pinch of inflation and this year the concerts were no longer free. They cost three to six dollars.

At my house, too, things are different this Christmas—and things are the same. Nina's son Claudie/Chuck, who has been coming to my Christmas dinner since he was eleven, will be coming tomorrow in uniform, on holiday leave from the U.S. Marine Corps. My refrigerator hasn't grown, however, so as usual, my dessert is in the freezer of 16-B, and my sweet-potato casserole is in the refrigerator of 4-F. And though the two girls who lived up the hall in 8-E are both married now, one of them still lives there, with her husband, and after dinner Richard will wheel my tea wagon full of dishes up the hall to be put in 8-E's dishwasher. Chester, his Old English sheepdog, and Duke, Nina's German shepherd who was my own true love, are both dead now. But Bentley, the abandoned sheepdog Richard adopted, is coming to dinner, and he'll trot up the hall alongside the tea wagon as the other dogs used to.

Merry Christmas. And a Happy New Year to you all.

NINETEEN EIGHTY-ONE

1981

JANUARY

My friend Arlene is not a dog lover. Which is the least of the
differences that make us the world's unlikeliest best friends.
To begin with, she's twenty years younger than I. To continue, she's been twice married and divorced, while I've been
single all my life.

Like me, she presently lives alone. But I live alone in a
studio apartment, consisting of a living room with functional
modern furniture and a small alcove for my desk, typewriter
table and bookshelves. And Arlene lives alone in an eight-
room penthouse, with a bedroom suitably decorated for
Marie Antoinette, and a living room positively alive with silver
and china ornaments and glittering chandeliers.

To round out the picture, I am plain and mousy, while
Arlene is black-haired, flamboyantly beautiful, and the last
word in high-fashion *chic*. But we're the same size. And since
Arlene wouldn't dream of wearing the same wardrobe two
years running, she gives me her designer suits at the end of
each year and I wear them for the next eight.

Her apartment house is up at the far end of my block, but
Arlene has always led a high-powered social life; and in the
years when I sat out on the front step with Nina and Richard

63

and their two dogs, Duke, the German shepherd, and Chester, the Old English sheepdog, Arlene never saw me there. When I tried to tell her about Duke and Chester and their canine friends, she always cut in firmly with: "I don't want to hear about your dogs."

But through me, Arlene did become friends with Nina and Richard. And when she and they came to my house for dinner on Thanksgiving and Christmas, Arlene was resigned to having Duke and Chester as her fellow dinner guests. When both dogs died two years ago, she was genuinely distressed, for our sakes, but she didn't exactly miss them.

And so, this Thanksgiving Richard called me early in the day. Should he bring Bentley to dinner? "Of course you're bringing Bentley to dinner!" I said. I hadn't told Arlene about Bentley, but he was coming to Thanksgiving dinner, and Arlene would just have accept him.

That evening Bentley—who is a huge, snowy mop of a dog—was at the door to greet her when Arlene arrived, wearing a flame-colored shimmering blouse and high black storm trooper's boots with six-inch heels. While Richard made the drinks, I was busy passing hors d'oeuvres and checking on everything in the kitchen, so it was some time before I settled down with my drink and glanced at Arlene.

She was sitting on the sofa, Bentley at her feet sitting with his back to her and his head locked in a vise between her high black storm trooper boots. As Richard and I gawked at her, Arlene yanked Bentley's head back, peered down into his eyes—one brown, one blue—and informed him:

"I like you. You're a very sophisticated dog."

Bentley was clearly ecstatic at the mauling, but I said: "Bite her, Bentley," whereupon Arlene pulled his head back further, pried his jaws open and stuck her fist in his mouth.

"No dog has ever crossed the threshold of my penthouse,"

she told him. "But you're special. You're coming to my New Year's Eve party."

A week later, invitations went out to fifty people—and one dog—to a New Year's Eve breakfast at Arlene's, to begin at 2:30 a.m. and run till sunrise. Richard went early, to help Arlene, so Bentley, wearing a formal black bow tie, was on hand to greet the first guests. Since he took up the entire foyer, the guests couldn't move beyond the front door till Bentley led them into the living room, which he did. Between arrivals, Bentley circulated, sitting with first one group and then another, now and then going to the bar to refresh himself at the sterling silver water bowl Arlene had set down for him, on the floor next to the champagne bucket.

I also went to the party—kicking and screaming—having been hounded by my hostess into staying up for it. I left at quarter to four and went home to bed. Bentley had to see every departing guest to the door, he didn't get home till eight a.m. and he spent the next two days sleeping it off.

So, of course, did Arlene. So it wasn't till the third day that she phoned to discuss the party.

"People have been phoning all day," she said. "Would you like to know what they talked about? Never mind the gorgeous buffet table, never mind the champagne. Never mind the great piano player. Never mind I looked sensational. All anybody talked about was Bentley. Will you tell me how I can be bananas over a dog who took the stage away from me at my own party?"

FEBRUARY

For at least eighty or ninety years, New York City has been honoring the nation's heroes with a parade that is unique. Drawing its name from its unique feature, it's called a ticker-tape parade.

The parade always begins in the old, original City of New York, in Lower Manhattan, because that's where the stock exchange is, and the parade's name comes from stock market ticker tape, a narrow strip of paper tape on which stock prices are recorded, which flows from ticker-tape machines all day long. The day before the parade, brokerage office workers save the day's accumulation of ticker tape and during the parade, as the heroes—standing or sitting in open cars—ride slowly by in the street below, the office workers fling the ticker tape out of their skyscraper windows, to stream down on the heroes' bare heads in a fine paper blizzard. So a ticker-tape parade requires only three things: ticker tape, open cars, and open windows.

But times change. To begin with, though ticker tape is still in use, it's being steadily replaced by office computer screens recording stock prices electronically, so that where there were once five hundred ticker-tape machines, there are now ninety. To continue, car manufacturers don't make open cars any more. And to conclude, office skyscrapers built here in the past decade have year-round air-conditioning called climate control, and their windows don't open.

You don't suppose a mere triple shortage of ticker tape, open cars and open windows was going to keep New York from throwing a ticker-tape parade for the American hostages home from Iran? Please.

First, the city administration dug up and dusted off two open cars, a 1930 Packard and a 1952 Chrysler convertible, it borrowed two custom-made Rolls-Royces from patriotic millionaires, and still not having enough open cars, it hoisted remaining hostages onto the roofs of closed cars. Next, it ordered five hundred miles of confetti to be distributed to the crowds lining the parade route. The skyscraper office workers, not to be outdone, collected computer printouts, tore up IBM cards, and shredded telephone books for their traditional paper blizzard. And in skyscrapers where the windows don't open, the workers just went up on the roof—fifty or sixty or ninety stories above the street—and threw their ersatz ticker tape from there.

I watched the parade on television, and it was something to see, not only for the faces of the hostages but for the people— a half million of them—packed deep along the route, wearing yellow bows and yellow ribbons, carrying banners reading "Welcome Home" and "U.S.A. 52 - Iran O," cheering and laughing and crying and linking arms in an outpouring of patriotism that caught us all up in it, and took all of us by surprise. Somehow, as the long years of Vietnam and Watergate had divided the country and made us ashamed, the simple everyday valor of the hostages united us and made us proud. That's the conclusion my friend Richard and I came to, anyway.

Speaking of Richard, Bentley wishes to thank all the "Woman's Hour" listeners who sent him Christmas greetings through me. I wish to report that though he lived in Vermont until his family abandoned him, Bentley is now a confirmed New Yorker. Richard says the conversion began on Bentley's first evening, when Richard took him around the block and then came back to our front step. Bentley sat bolt upright on the sidewalk in front of the step, gawking at the steady stream of dogs and people, cabs and cars and buses going by, at the blinking traffic lights and brightly lit store windows, with an expression that said "Where has all this been all my life?" And having grown up in a one-family house, as soon as Bentley discovered that our building contained a dizzying number of homes and families, he took to getting on the elevator by himself, when Richard wasn't looking, ready to go visiting wherever it stopped.

But your childhood home is your childhood home, and there are memories. We had a snowstorm last month, when the gutters were still piled with discarded Christmas trees. The snow concealed some of the ragged branches, and clumps of it dotted all of them. And every time Bentley went around the block in the next day or two, he stopped at each bedraggled tree, his nose deep in the snow-laden branches, which he snuffed lingeringly. Watching him, you knew he was remembering the pine woods and snowy winters of Vermont.

MARCH

I wish to enlist your sympathy for the poor millionaires who live on Fifth Avenue, in New York's most expensive town houses and co-op apartments. With the coming of the warm months, they're braced for a long succession of parades up Fifth Avenue, Sunday after Sunday.

These parades are ethnic. Take the Pulaski Day and von Steuben Day parades, in honor of European generals who fought in our War of Independence. Pulaski was a Pole, von Steuben was German, so the Pulaski Day parade is organized by Polish New Yorkers, the von Steuben Day parade by German New Yorkers. There are parades on Greek Independence Day, Puerto Rico Day, Salute to Israel Day, Philippine Independence Day, and so forth, including Captive Nations Day, for Armenian, Bulgarian, Czech, Hungarian, Lithuanian and Rumanian New Yorkers.

All these parades go straight up Fifth Avenue, which means that at eight a.m. of a spring Sunday, the occupants of a town house are wakened by the boom-boom of the drum and the raucous blare of a trumpet, as the first marching band tunes up under their windows. It will be followed by twenty more marching bands and the millionaires will get no peace for the rest of the day.

The millionaires formed community action groups and

demanded that the city issue parade permits only on week-days. But this was fought by Fifth Avenue merchants, since parade crowds impede shoppers and are bad for business. So the millionaires demanded that the city move its Sunday parades to some other avenue. This the city could not do. You can't give one ethnic group the right to march up Fifth Avenue and tell all other groups to march somewhere else.

And a century ago, the first ethnic group to hold a parade had its right to use Fifth Avenue written into the city charter. That group still holds the city's biggest and most popular parade, popular even with the millionaires since it's never on a Sunday. The parade is held on March 17 (and when that falls on a Sunday it's held on the 18th) because the parade is in honor of St. Patrick's Day, with a reviewing stand in front of St. Patrick's Cathedral.

St. Patrick's Day is unique in New York; for reasons known to nobody, on March 17, the entire city becomes Irish. Everybody wears a green tie or blouse to work and florists do a booming business in green buttonhole carnations. But I have to tell you about the one never-to-be-forgotten St. Patrick's Day, back in the sixties.

New York has always had a large Irish Catholic population and a small Irish Protestant population. But one year in the sixties, the Mayor of Dublin, Robert Briscoe, was to be guest of honor at the St. Patrick's Day parade and the newspapers announced that Robert Briscoe was not an Irish Catholic nor yet an Irish Protestant, but—Heaven bless us—an Irish Jew. I mean to tell you, the Jewish population of New York went completely out of its mind.

Cohen's clothing store and Goldberg's Meat Market painted green O-apostrophes on their signs and became O'Cohen's and O'Goldberg's for the day. Delicatessens sold green bagels, kosher restaurants served green matzo-balls and green noodles in their soup. Whole Hebrew schools turned out for *that* parade as the annual sea of green floats, marching bands, and schoolgirls in green shorts rolled past the Cathedral before the three dignitaries on the reviewing stand: Jewish Mayor Briscoe of Dublin, and Protestant Mayor Lindsay of New York with the Catholic cardinal between them.

Well, this year's St. Patrick's Day parade has just come and gone, and the long Sunday parade season looms ahead. Which brings us back to the millionaires. Why do they put up with it? Why don't they move?

They'll keep fighting to have the parades moved to some other day or some other avenue. But they know that those ethnic parades, which would be unimaginable in any other great city in the world are the essence of this one, the visible signs of that melting pot out of which New York was created. They know it because the millionaires, too, are descended from poor immigrants, beckoned here by the statue in the harbor, holding out hope of a better life. So the millionaires and the marchers are all kin—all New Yorkers—like the rest of us.

APRIL

A few weeks ago, I got a letter from a woman in London. "We hear awful reports of the danger of walking around New York at night," she wrote. "How do you manage? Do you carry a hat pin?"

Two days later, I got on line at Saks Fifth Avenue's information desk, in time to overhear two Englishmen in front of me express disbelief that Saks didn't carry the item they wanted. They turned away, and, wanting to be helpful, I hurried after them.

"Gentlemen," I said, "what is it you want to buy?" One of the men pointed to my shoulder bag.

"The gadget you women carry in your handbags to repel muggers," he said. I told him I'd never heard of such a gadget, and he said flatly: "Every woman in New York carries one."

What I answered, I'll tell you in a minute. First, you need to know geographically what is, and is not, New York.

When you visualize New York City, you rightly see the city on Manhattan Island, a narrow strip twelve miles long by less than two miles wide. But it's surrounded by four other cities, three of them much larger than itself. And back in 1898, for political reasons, the four other cities merged with New York City to create a paper monolith called Greater New York. And because "Greater" elsewhere means a string of suburbs around a single city, let me be plain about what constitutes Greater New York.

Of the five cities included, the largest is Brooklyn. As many people live in the city of Brooklyn as live in the city of Paris. Next comes Queens, with a population larger than that of Vienna. Add the Bronx, with more people than Warsaw; Staten Island, with more people than Cardiff; and New York City—Manhattan—with as many people as live in Greater Liverpool with all its suburbs.

Like any city, Brooklyn has its well-to-do neighborhoods and its slums. So does Queens. The Bronx splits into the burnt-out slums of the South Bronx and the upper income suburbs of the North Bronx, which also has small estates, rolling green acres dotted with palatial homes and expensive private schools.

Ask people in those places where they live and they'll answer "Brooklyn," or "Forest Hills," which is in Queens, or "Riverdale," in the North Bronx. If they're coming into Manhattan for the day, ask them where they're going and they'll answer: "To New York." To them, as to you, New York is the city on Manhattan Island.

Which brings us to crime. Brooklyn, Queens, the Bronx and New York City all have high crime rates. But, as the world knows, I live in a violent country. Each year a national police report is published listing the cities with the highest per-capita crime rates. During the last few years of the seventies, the American city with the highest crime rate was Phoenix, Arizona. In 1980, Miami was first, Phoenix dropped to second. New York City on Manhattan Island was eighteenth.

Then why does the world think of New York City as the crime capital of the world? Well, the statistics don't please the news media. How can you get sensational headlines from crime in Phoenix, Arizona? How can you paint a lurid picture on television of sunny Miami as the new Babylon? It's much easier to use bad old New York.

So the media reporters ignore everyday crime elsewhere and instead tot up (and publicize) every crime committed in Brooklyn, Queens, the Bronx, Staten Island and New York City and present the total to you as "crime in New York," knowing that you'll read it as crime in New York City on Manhattan Island which is the only New York you plan to visit. They do it because it makes a better story that way. But it's as misleading as if they'd totted up the crime totals for Paris, Vienna, Warsaw, Cardiff and Greater Liverpool—and presented the total to you as crime in Liverpool.

To the lady in London: no, I don't carry a hat pin. Like all my friends, I walk alone at night through every neighborhood on the Upper East Side, and every neighborhood in midtown except the Times Square area, which is now a slum. And I would no more walk alone through a New York slum at night than you would walk alone through a Paris or Liverpool slum at night. And all I could think of to say to the Englishman who informed me that "every woman in New

York" carries an anti-mugging gadget no woman I know ever heard of, was:

"You've been reading too many newspapers."

MAY

It's a beautiful spring here, and I've been spending late afternoons walking in Central Park, as I will through October. My friend Arlene, on the other hand, has never set foot in Central Park, though she enjoys driving through it in a cab. Neither her Chanel pumps with the pogo-stick heels, nor her chic designer suits were made for Central Park.

Central Park is very unlike English parks. In April, when the pink and white cherry blossoms are out, and the four hundred acres of green are empty and quiet, it might remind you of Hyde Park—until you passed the toddlers' play-grounds, the baseball diamonds and the tennis courts. But it's not till the first warm weekend in May that Central Park becomes what one songwriter called it: the Big Back Yard of the City. Walk across any of its lawns on a warm Sunday and you'll come upon a burly truck driver stretched out on the grass, sunbathing in nothing but his shorts, his wife curled up beside him asleep, her faded sundress riding all the way up to here. And why not? They're in their own backyard. Walking in the park on a warm weekend afternoon, you pass countless family picnics, Frisbee games and youthful musicians playing jazz or marimba or chamber music. Not to mention the joggers, roller skaters and bikers. When you're tired of walking, you climb Dog Hill and watch an international assortment of dogs race around the quarter-mile stretch of New York's canine social center. And if a small dog drops a wet ball in your lap or a large dog rests a paw on your shoulder, it doesn't matter: you're wearing your old backyard clothes. Unless you're me and your best friend is Arlene.

Arlene leads a high-powered professional life, which I'll tell you about sometime because I'm involved in it. She also leads a high-powered social life. What she used to do every year was donate a sizable part of her wardrobe to the neighborhood thrift shops—second-hand clothing stores run by charities. Then she met me and discovered that I was exactly her size and had, from where she stood, no clothes. I don't look well in her dresses. But on the day I first tried on Arlene's pants and jackets—which she buys by the ton—the thrift shops lost an annual fortune in designer pant-suits.

Arlene wears them for a season and gives them to me and I wear them for the next six. I have only one large wardrobe closet, and in no time I had to throw out my own clothes to make room for the avalanche of hers. I started wearing three-hundred-dollar pants to Central Park because I no longer owned any other kind.

For a while the results burdened my conscience. Duke was going to the park with me in those days, and on a summer day I'd find myself standing in Central Park Lake, with Jaeger's finest linen pants rolled up and splattered, as I fished Duke's muddy sticks out of the shallows and threw them back for him to chase again. And there was the autumn day when we were playing tug-of-war and I fell and ripped the knee in one of Bill Blass's finest wool pants. But you don't change your life to suit your wardrobe. I just told myself philosophically they were only my second-best black pants and I didn't like black anyway. You get used to anything—especially yourself.

But as my attitude toward her wardrobe became cavalier, her attitude became preposterous. A couple of years ago, just before I was to leave for London, I came home one afternoon to find the phone ringing. I answered it, and Arlene said:

"Where were you all day? I've been trying to get you."

"I was downtown buying a raincoat for London," I said. And her voice came wailing over the wire:

"Why didn't you *tell* me you needed a raincoat? I have raincoats!"

"I just thought it would be nice," I told her, "if I *bought* something I needed, for a change!"

Would you like to know what she said in a disapproving tone? With thousands of dollars' worth of clothes she'd barely worn, hanging in my closet? She said:

"You're extravagant."

AUGUST

Hi, I'm back. And my heartfelt thanks to all the kind "Woman's Hour" listeners who phoned their concern to the BBC and sent me "Get Well" wishes. I'll tell you why I was in the hospital in a minute. First, two Royal Wedding notes.

You probably know that New York is the home of the garment industry known to its workers as "the Rag trade." Well, from five a.m. on July 29—which is when the wedding was seen over here—straight round the clock till five a.m. of July 30, New York's garment industry worked to copy the Royal Wedding dress in several variations of fabric, headdress and train length, to fit several price ranges, in response to an avalanche of telephone orders for the dress from department stores and dress shops all over this far-flung country. Just in case you were wondering whether Americans were interested in the Royal Wedding.

But no Americans were quite so interested as those who work for *Women's Wear Daily*. *Women's Wear Daily*—known as *WWD*—is the newspaper and Bible of the garment industry. In addition to its packed pages of fashion news, *Women's Wear*

Daily prints reviews and gossip columns, and through them it has acquired a reputation for being abrasive, for sniping at celebrities it dislikes, and thus for making enemies. Well, the story goes that on the morning of July 28 the first editor to arrive at the *WWD* offices found that a sketch of the top-secret Royal Wedding dress had been slipped under the door by an anonymous donor. The staff worked feverishly, all that day and night, to enlarge, photograph and describe the dress for the next day's issue. Not till five a.m. on July 29 did *WWD* turn on its TV set and discover the hoax: it had been given a sketch of the wrong dress. Moral: it does not pay to make enemies.

My friend Maxine, a native New Yorker who's lived in Los Angeles for years, was in town last week, and coming from an area where people live in widely separated houses, scattered among canyons, she made a discovery about New York.

"This city," she announced, "is a Life Support System. You may be alone, but you're never isolated. Walk out on the street, at any hour, day or night, and there's life, everywhere."

I knew that better than she did. What I was doing in the hospital was having cataract surgery on both eyes. Since I'd been very nearsighted, I recovered a great deal of my sight after surgery, but I couldn't see print at all. When I say I couldn't read or write, I mean I couldn't read a telephone dial, or the numbers on elevator buttons, and I couldn't write a grocery list since I couldn't see my own handwriting. The apartment house I live in was my first Support System. In-house friends and neighbors did my marketing, brought me the mail I couldn't read and paid my bills by writing checks for me and putting a finger on the line where I had to sign them. But it was the boredom of idleness that was the hardest to bear, till my eyes were able to face the outdoor light. Then I began going down to the front step, to sit for hours watching the "life everywhere" go by.

Sitting there, I found I could see traffic lights and curbstones clearly and that gave me the courage to walk to Central Park by myself, and then down Fifth Avenue by myself. In the two months of waiting for my eyes to heal, I walked endlessly, all over this Life Support System city.

Whereupon it turned out that print wasn't the only thing I couldn't see. There was the day I saw a man coming toward me with a collie on leash. Not till they came within a few feet of me did I discover that the "collie" was a large brown and white suitcase. Never mind; it was bliss, one fine June Saturday, to sail down Fifth Avenue in my best suit, even though I wasn't going anywhere, since I couldn't see well enough to go shopping. And when I got down to 54th Street and saw ahead of me, at 53rd, the spires of St. Thomas's Church, I decided maybe I was going somewhere after all. St. Thomas's is famous for the concerts of its marvelous men's and boys' choirs; and when I saw a large pink banner billowing down the front steps, I hurried toward it, hoping somehow to see what was being advertised. I came to a small crowd as I neared the church, so I detoured down to the curb just as a limousine door opened and a bride stepped out and walked straight into me. That's when I discovered that the billowing pink banner was a line of six pink bridesmaids.

I fled to the far side steps of the church. Then I crept up the steps, opened the far side door, tiptoed down the far side aisle—and went to the wedding.

SEPTEMBER

Big excitement here a couple of weeks ago because *The New York Times* ran a story about Arlene, with a photograph of her that also included Richard.

Since you know that Arlene and I are opposites, when I tell you that I detest large cocktail parties and dinner dances, you won't be surprised to learn that Arlene earns her living organizing large cocktail parties and dinner dances. She runs the parties as fund-raising events for Democratic politicians who need money for their election campaigns. Her most famous fund raiser was a birthday party for the mayor of New York aboard the *Queen Elizabeth II*—"the *Q.E. Two*" to Arlene. She phoned the office of the ship's public relations chief, who was "at sea" off the Bermuda coast, and via ship-to-shore phone she talked him into letting her hire the ship for the mayor's birthday party. She hypnotized the chef into creating a replica of New York's City Hall in margarine and a birthday cake bigger than the undersized mayor.

Then there was the dinner for the mayor when he retired. Arlene was determined to snag President Carter as guest of honor. But Carter was due in New York expressly to attend a performance at the Metropolitan Opera that evening. So Arlene commandeered the Grand Promenade deck of the Met for a gala dinner before the opera, and the assembled guests—including the President—were assured of getting to the opera on time afterward.

It's a one-woman business, but I'm involved in it. I write her invitations. I slave over them. Arlene tailors each party to the personality or status of the client, so one invitation must be funny, another elegant, a third trendy-chic. And we spend hours choosing the right colors and print styles. Most of her clients have their own staffs who can work the party: sit at the reservations table, take tickets at the door and keep out gate-crashers. But when the client has no staff, or one Arlene considers inefficient, I work the reservations table and Richard is ticket taker and bouncer. Which is how we both happened to be at her latest party, a couple of weeks ago, and it was fabulous. A Moonlight Sail and Supper-Dance, it said on the invitation—a three-hour cruise around Manhattan Island, on a double-decker wooden tourist boat, which Arlene transformed with flower-decked small tables around a long buffet opulent with mounds of lobster, shrimp and poached salmon and cornucopias of summer salad and summer fruits.

There were two bars and two dance orchestras, one on each deck, but the chief attraction of the cruise was the New York skyline, with its thousands of pinpoint lights and the heart-stopping sight of the Statue of Liberty, floodlit in gold and so close we felt we could almost reach out and touch her arm.

The *Times* photographer wanted to show Arlene serving lobster to guests, but since the picture was taken before the guests arrived, the ersatz "guests" in it were Richard and Arlene's father. (I declined; I hate having my picture taken.) The next morning I rushed out to get the *Times*, but the corner newsstand was sold out. He denies it, but I claim Richard bought out the stock, to send his picture-in-the-*Times* to all his relatives back home in Pennsylvania.

I am happy to report that Bentley, Richard's Old English sheepdog, is now a champion, with all the requisite blue ribbons to prove it. It took nine months of dog shows, which didn't bother Bentley, but took a lot out of Richard. He spent almost every weekend driving Bentley to dog shows in Ohio, Virginia, Vermont, Massachusetts. It usually meant a five-hundred-mile round trip, but it wasn't the driving that wore Richard out; it was Bentley.

Bentley likes cars, but he has strong views on how they ought to behave. He thinks cars should (a) be quiet, and (b) keep moving. Being a very large sheepdog, Bentley has a deafening bark. And during the weekly five-hundred-mile trip, every time Richard honked his horn, Bentley barked; every time Richard turned on the windshield wiper, Bentley barked; and every time the car got stuck in traffic, Bentley barked. By June, when Bentley finally became a champion—in fine health and spirits—Richard had developed psychosomatic rheumatism and stomach trouble. He's only just recovering.

OCTOBER

I told you this is the season when New Yorkers redecorate apartments, replenish wardrobes and drive to the country to see the foliage. In all of these activities, tenants in our building have the assistance of two enterprising doormen and one enterprising superintendent. All three men, wanting more for their families than their paychecks will buy, have found ways to earn a little money on the side.

Paul, the doorman, for instance, runs a one-man limousine service all year round. He drives tenants to and from airports and to and from vacation resorts. He's such a careful and chivalrous driver that the building's old ladies won't go to the seashore in the summer until Paul is free to drive them. But he's also a rabid scenery lover. Every spring he dials a phone operator in Mobile, Alabama, to ask when the azaleas are at their height, and he dials a Virginia operator to find out when the Shenandoah apple blossoms are in bloom. So of course he's an expert on autumn foliage.

"The foliage," he told me, "starts at the Canadian-New England border the first chilly day in September, and moves south at the rate of fifty miles—seventy kilometers—a week." In October, he can always tell tenants where the foliage is at its peak, and he's available to drive them there on his days off.

Then there's Tony, another doorman, whose sideline is Selling Things. You come home one night and see piled on the front desk a row of gaudy-awful statuettes, vases, oil paintings and china ornaments which Tony wants to sell you to brighten your apartment. A week or two later, these dubious home furnishings are gone, replaced by shirts, blouses and sweaters at bargain prices. They're not the finest quality but Tony is young and handsome, and we have lots of pretty young female tenants who are glad to buy a T-shirt or a blouse to oblige him.

Finally, there's Danny, our super, who, with a second baby on the way, built window boxes for Nina's terrace last summer. Last week he offered to paint my kitchen and bathroom for a fair price, and in my innocence I was overjoyed. I knew he'd do a better job than the painters supplied by the building's owners since in New York, the phrase "landlord's paint" means the cheapest, poorest quality paint available. I told Danny I wanted both rooms painted plain white as usual, and he drove all the way down to the Lower East Side to buy the best paint. He spent a long morning painting my tiny kitchen and tinier bathroom, and when I saw the results I had to admit that it was the cleanest, most careful paint job I'd ever had. But, not being a professional, Danny knew nothing about mixing paint. My kitchen walls are so glittering, glossy white they're positively blinding. And the screaming white bathroom walls turned the bathroom tiles a dingy yellow by comparison. Now he wants to paint the living room, and I haven't yet figured out how to handle the problem.

I have a small item for you about my friend Arlene and her love affair with Bentley, the sheepdog. But first you have to know that New York's banking industry has gone completely round-the-bend. Every bank is offering such a wide assortment of gifts, to induce you to open an account that its once-dignified interior now resembles a flea market. For a ten-thousand-dollar deposit, you can get a free food processor; for a five-thousand-dollar-deposit, a free radio or camera—and so on down the line. And when a bank opens a new branch in your neighborhood, you may get a gift just for walking inside, though these gifts are of the worthless kind known in New York as "schlock." Which brings us to Arlene and Bentley.

Arlene phoned Richard last Saturday night to say that she had dinner guests who had been charmed by Bentley at her New Year's Eve breakfast and wanted to see him again. "Bring him over," said Arlene. (She invites women to her house; men, she summons. If you look like Arlene, you can do that.) Richard obediently walked up the block to Arlene's apartment house with Bentley, who, like any other male, lets Arlene maul him around.

And so, late that night when I went across the street to the newsstand to get my Sunday *Times* and met Richard and Bentley getting their Sunday *Times,* Bentley was surrounded by an admiring throng of newspaper buyers, because he was wearing a present from Arlene. His vast, furry sheepdog bulk was covered by an outsized blue T-shirt, emblazoned with large black letters reading MANUFACTURERS HANOVER BANK.

NOVEMBER

If you come to New York and stay at a hotel on a street lined with apartment houses instead of office buildings, you may see a peculiar sight. Coming back to your hotel late one evening, you'll see cars parked on both sides of the street, and you may notice that many of the cars on one side of the street have drivers in them. The drivers are just sitting there, and you might assume they're waiting for passengers. They're not. They're waiting for a parking space on the opposite side of the street. They are victims of a New York City rule known as Alternate Side of the Street Parking.

Our sanitation trucks—lorries—can't clean the streets properly if cars are parked on both sides of them. So every few days cars on one side of the street have to be moved to the other side. Well, you park your car on a Monday, knowing you'll have to move it before eight a.m. on Thursday. If you wait till seven-thirty on Thursday morning, you may have to drive all over the neighborhood and settle for a parking space several blocks away. So instead, at ten or eleven o'clock on Wednesday evening, you go down and sit in your car. Since it's parked on your own block, you know at a glance which cars on the opposite side of the street belong to neighbors and which belong to visiting dinner guests, and you just sit and wait till one of the visitors drives off and leaves you a parking space. Or you know, through the grapevine, which car-owning doormen go off duty at midnight, and you wait for one of the parking spaces they'll leave behind. But if you're resourceful, you make good use of your waiting time.

Alan, Susan's husband up the hall in 8-E, has a growing library in his car; that's where he does most of his reading. And Joanie, with record-playing teenagers in the house, keeps stationery and pens in the glove compartment; car-sitting gives her a chance to write letters in peace and quiet.

And now I hope you'll forgive an entirely personal item. I can't talk about anything else because I can't think about anything else. These talks are taped at the BBC studio in New York a few days before they're broadcast. Which is how it happens that while you're listening to my voice, I'm flying over the Atlantic on my way to London. And thereby hangs a miraculous true story.

When I was young, I believed I was born to be a great playwright, and my favorite daydream was of attending the gala opening night of one of my plays. As things turned out, I wrote very bad plays that nobody ever produced, and the daydream went the way of most youthful dreams. But at the same age, I had a second dream. This one was to see, someday, the England of English literature—and especially London. Since the trip was out of the question on a struggling writer's income, I did the next-best thing: I established a link with literary England by ordering books from Marks & Company, an antiquarian bookshop in London. For twenty years, I corresponded with one man at the bookstore, Frank Doel. When, in 1969, he died suddenly, my sense of grief and loss drove me to write the story of our correspondence in a small book, using as its title the address of the bookshop: *84, Charing Cross Road.* It would take a volume to tell you the ways in which that little book transformed my life. But for a start, when André Deutsch published the book in England, the second of my youthful dreams came true: I made the trip to London for publication day.

A few years later, the BBC adapted the book for television, which gave me another trip to London. Then BBC radio got into the act and invited me to do a broadcast once a month, to tell you about everyday life in New York. Which brings us to the crowning touch—and the reason why I'm flying over the Atlantic on my way to London again.

A man named James Roose-Evans—whom I've yet to meet—adapted *84, Charing Cross Road* for the stage. Another man named Michael Redington—whom I've yet to meet— decided to produce the play at a London West End theatre. Wherefore, on Thursday, November 26, I'll be going to the Ambassador Theatre to attend that gala Opening Night I daydreamed about, almost a lifetime ago.

And as if the people involved in the production knew all this and carefully chose the most appropriate possible date for the opening, would you believe that Thursday, November 26, is that special holiday in the American calendar, known as Thanksgiving Day?

NINETEEN EIGHTY-TWO

1982

JANUARY

If you lose the door keys to your house, you can climb in a window. If you lose the door keys to your apartment, you are locked out and you have to call a locksmith who charges the earth to break the latch or the double lock and install new ones. So most apartment house tenants keep a set of spare keys, and our building provides a wall safe for them, in the lobby package room. You might therefore suppose that all my neighbors' spare keys are hanging on hooks in the wall safe. You would be wrong. I live in 8-G and attached to the hook with my spare keys is a note:

"Please give my keys to any tenant in 8-A, 8-E, 8-F, or 8-I who gets locked out." Their spare keys are in my apartment.

First, there's Carol, next door in 8-F. Carol is young, pretty and suspicious. She believes that if she left her keys in the lobby safe, the super might sneak up and steal her furniture while she was out. (According to the super, there's at least one such suspicious tenant on every floor.) There there's Dimitria, across the hall from me in 8-I. Dimitria's young daughter Steffi used to lose her keys regularly, so Dimitria, who'd never had spare keys, had a set made for me. Thereafter, when Steffi lost her keys, it was my job to hound her into having new ones made and returning the spares to me before she lost *them*. Steffi is now very grown up and living in London, but I still have Dimitria's keys; I'm closer than the lobby if she gets locked out. Next come Susan and Alan, in 8-E, who go on ski vacations in winter and beach vacations in summer. I have their keys because I'm in charge of watering their plants when they're away. Which I don't mind, since along with the plants I also get custody of their dishwasher.

Which brings us to 8-A. I wouldn't know the tenant in 8-A, much less have her keys, if it weren't for Blue Eyes. Blue Eyes is a Persian cat.

Our floors are L-shaped. I live at the top of the L, and Carol, Dimitria, Susan and Alan all live on the long hall with me. But 8-A is at the other end of the L, on the short hall, and I didn't know who lived there till the evening I heard a meowing in the hall, and opened my door to see a distraught Persian cat who had obviously got locked out. I invited him in and while I buzzed the lobby to ask who on my floor owned a cat, my guest jumped happily from the sofa to the rocker to the phone table. The doorman told me there were two cats in 8-A, but my visitor was in no hurry to leave. I finally caught him and told him I didn't like cats (I'm a dog-lover), but he purred broad-mindedly in my arms all the way to 8-A. When I rang the bell, a middle-aged blonde opened the door. She'd gone to the incinerator, not knowing that Blue Eyes had followed her; that's how he got locked out. She told me her own name was Blossom, that she was supervisor of the night emergency room at a nearby hospital and would take special care of me if I ever was taken there in the night, and we parted. It was some weeks before I saw her again. We came up in the elevator together one Saturday afternoon, and Blossom said bluntly:

"You're not gonna believe this! Every morning at six a.m. when I come home from work and let myself in, my Blue Eyes shoots out and all the way around to your door, and scratches and meows to be let in. He's in love with you!"

I sleep till seven, so I'd never heard him, but I said I thought he was entitled to come and see me and ten minutes later, Blossom, Blue Eyes and his sister, Puss, arrived for a state visit. Puss hid under the sofa, but Blue Eyes was ecstatic, rolling in my lap and purring till he almost slobbered. ("I'm so jealous!" said Blossom. "He never slobbers over me!") After that, they came for a ten-minute visit most Saturdays.

So it was natural for Blossom to ring my doorbell when a crisis arose, early one Sunday morning. She had gone out to the incinerator—in her ample, diaphanous pink nightgown— only to hear her front door blow shut, locking her out. I buzzed the lobby and while Blossom hid in my apartment, the porter got her spare keys from the safe, brought them up and unlocked her door—looking mystified when he didn't see her anywhere. When he left, Blossom's spare keys got transferred from the lobby safe to the lazy Susan on my desk.

The lazy Susan has little compartments marked "paper clips," "rubber bands" and so forth and the one marked "keys" is so stuffed with my neighbors' door keys there isn't room in it for the keys to my suitcases. I have to keep them in the compartment marked "what-not."

FEBRUARY

I don't know whether her use of the term is medically accurate, but a friend of mine, housebound during this cold winter, described herself as having "cabin fever." Thinking about this, I decided that in her meaning of the phrase, our whole building has been suffering from cabin fever. The symptoms appear in our paranoid reactions to everyday irritations we normally put up with.

Take the Quarter problem. A quarter is a coin worth one-fourth of a dollar, and our basement laundry, having doubled its prices to a dollar for the washer and a dollar for the dryer, installed new machines with coin slots that accept *only* quarters. So you need four quarters for the washer and four for the dryer, and if you have to go downtown by bus, you need six more quarters—three each for the trip down and back. Now it's hard enough just to assemble fourteen quarters on any given day. But the company that owns the washers and dryers makes matters worse by not emptying the machines' receiving trays often enough. So one day you put your four quarters in the slot, and the receiving tray, already overloaded with quarters, jams. You not only can't operate the machine; you don't get your quarters back. You summon the handyman, who tells you to phone the company, they'll send you a one-dollar refund check. Normally, you say testily: "That won't get my laundry done, will it!" This winter, one woman threw her laundry at the handyman, and I marched upstairs and phoned the Consumer Protection Bureau.

Then there's the incinerator, which is now a compactor but is still called the incinerator from the days when it burned up our garbage instead of compressing it. The incinerator is a hand-operated bin in a hall closet on every floor. Well, now and then a floor has one tenant who, instead of using the incinerator, leaves bags of wet garbage on the hall carpet outside it. Normally, this leads, at most, to an anonymous note taped to the incinerator door. There's the polite note: "Will whoever left garbage on the hall carpet PLEASE put it down the incinerator hereafter? So we're not overrun with cockroaches?" And there's the rude note: "Mrs. Zilch. You and your filthy garbage are being reported to the Department of Sanitation."

The "Mrs. Zilch" means that the writer went through a bag of garbage to locate an empty envelope or discarded bill

revealing the identity of the culprit. Well, on my friend Richard's floor, this situation was also aggravated by cabin fever.

Richard's next door neighbors, the Zuckermans, are a dignified middle-aged lawyer and his friendly, unassuming wife. They had gone through the garbage of the floor's garbage pest and traced it to a young woman down the hall. The next day, Mrs. Zuckerman had rung the young woman's bell and appealed to her, but without results. Then one evening Richard heard voices raised in the hall, and opened his door to see Mr. Zuckerman and the young woman arguing. Mr. Zuckerman had caught her leaving a bag of wet garbage on the hall carpet, on her way out for the evening. He had followed her to the elevator, demanding that she dispose of her garbage, and she was refusing; she said the building's porters could do that. As Richard and Mrs. Zuckerman watched the argument, the elevator came. Mr. Zuckerman was barring the young woman's entrance to it, and she tried to push him out of her way. Whereupon he pushed her so hard she bounced against the opposite wall. And Mrs. Zuckerman protesting in horror:

"Sam, you're a *law*yer! You *assaulted* her! You're a *law*yer!"

Which brings us to the present—or impending—crisis. Last night a sign went up in the elevator, which goes up every time there's to be drilling in the street. The sign said that the building's water supply would be shut off today, from nine a.m. to five p.m., due to street repairs. "Please fill receptacles to give you an adequate water supply." So last night, before going to bed, the entire building filled its bathtubs and bathroom sinks, its stewpots, teakettles and scrub buckets. But at nine a.m. this morning, the water was not turned off. If the usual pattern is repeated, it won't be turned off tomorrow, either. But the sign will stay up in the elevator. And the

tenants, having long since emptied their receptacles, will grumble that the super ought to take the sign down.

And the day *after* tomorrow, everybody will wake up at seven a.m. to find the water turned off; nobody will have saved so much as a saucepan of water to wash or shave or brush teeth with, and the whole building will go berserk.

MARCH

One of the reasons why New York is such a stimulating place to live is that it fosters so many offbeat professions. I told you about my friend Arlene, who runs high-powered fund-raising parties for political candidates. My friend Judy is an actress in television commercials. She told me they call her "the Proctor & Gamble type"—meaning she's always cast as the young housewife, in TV ads for dishwasher detergents, paper diapers, oven cleaners, baby food, dog food, and—not inappropriately—headache pills. Judy has only one rehearsal for a commercial, and the rehearsal may run fifteen minutes or two hours. If she rehearses two hours for each of two commercials, she is paid—for four hours' work—more than a publisher pays me for a book which takes me six to twelve months to write. This is known as the law of supply and demand.

But if Judy is wildly overpaid for four hours' work, a gentleman in the building next door to mine makes almost as much money for doing no work at all. The gentleman owns a small dog and the *dog* appears in TV commercials. All the gentleman does is sit home and count the dog's money.

Which brings us to my friend Nina, who runs the dizziest one-woman cottage industry you ever watched operate. Like me, she's underpaid, so she has only a volunteer staff. But

Nina doesn't depend on her work for a living; she does it because she loves it. Nina designs and packages inexpensive gifts for cosmetics and housewares firms to give to their distributors and salespeople as Christmas gifts or promotional gifts or gifts to be handed out at the annual banquet. This is a perfectly normal job till you see it in action.

Nina has a studio across the street on the second floor of an old brownstone walk-up, a residential building where she is the only commercial tenant. The studio is one room, about fifteen feet square, but with a nine-foot-high ceiling and believe me, she needs it. When one of her clients wanted to introduce a new line of picnic products to his distributors, I walked into Nina's studio to find huge cartons, stacked clear to the ceiling, containing twelve hundred paper cups, twelve hundred paper plates and twelve hundred paper bowls—plus the twelve hundred paper chef's hats Nina had had made, accompanied by twelve hundred yellow buttons to be attached to the hats, each button bearing the words LE CUP—Nina's name for the new picnic line. For the next week, Nina's volunteers—an out-of-work magazine editor and two house-wives—unpacked the cartons and assembled each gift, one cup, plate, bowl, chef's hat and button, while Nina worked on the twelve hundred decorative drawstring sacks in which the gifts were to be packaged.

Then there was the client who wanted an inexpensive Easter gift for his representatives in fifty states, who were coming to town for Spring Market Week. Nina decided on small baskets containing three narcissus bulbs each. But the client had a thousand representatives. So there arrived at Nina's studio three thousand narcissus bulbs, two thousand pounds of gravel to pack them in, a thousand small baskets to hold the packed bulbs and a thousand florist's boxes to hold the baskets. This was last March, and it was cold in New York, but Nina and her helpers had to work in an unheated studio to keep the bulbs from blooming prematurely. ("I looked into one box of bulbs," Nina told me, "and saw this little head popping out! And I said: 'Girls, we're in trouble! Turn the radiator off.'"

Her latest completed project is still wearing off. A cosmetics firm wanted a gift for its several hundred Canadian sales-women, and Nina designed small packets of handmade sachets. She ordered fifty pounds of dried rose petals for the sachets, and then—to insure that the scent would survive the long trip to Canada—she sprayed the dried petals with essence of rose oil. She sprayed the fifty pounds of petals on a Friday afternoon. And when she came into the studio on Monday morning, the super had a story to tell her. He had waxed the building's floors on Saturday, as usual, and on Sunday, half the building's tenants had rung his doorbell to ask the name of the floor wax he'd used that made the halls smell like roses. For days that six-story building reeked of rose oil. Nina's studio, of course, still reeks of it two weeks later.

APRIL

This is the first April I can remember when the chief topic of conversation here has been the weather. But who could have imagined we'd all be flocking to Holy Week music services in fur coats and heavy boots, through snow-covered streets. My friend Bernadette and I went to several concerts at the big Fifth Avenue churches as usual. But on Holy Thursday, we went to a concert and service at a small church just off the avenue. And Bernadette was shocked that I'd never told you about it.

It's an Anglican church—the priest included your govern-ment as well as ours in his prayers—and officially, it's the

Church of the Transfiguration. But that's not the name by which New Yorkers know it. The story of its popular name goes back to a day in 1870.

New York even then was famous as a theatre capital. But in those days, men and women who appeared on the stage were considered beyond the pale socially. On a day in 1870 a famous comic actor named Joseph Jefferson, learning that a fellow actor had died, offered to make the funeral arrangements for the bereaved family and went to an imposing church on a corner of Madison Avenue to ask the minister to officiate at the dead actor's funeral.

"Oh, we couldn't possibly bury such a person from our church," said the minister. "But there's a little church around the corner that does that sort of thing." To which Joe Jefferson replied:

"Then God bless the little church around the corner!"

Word of this conversation spread through the theatre district in a matter of hours, and New York's most illustrious theatre names turned out for the actor's funeral at the Church of the Transfiguration, which was henceforth and forevermore to be known as the Little Church Around the Corner. Tallulah Bankhead was a parishioner there; Rex Harrison helped in its recent fund-raising drive. Memorial plaques and markers honor not only legendary American players—from Edwin Booth to Otis Skinner—but England's Gertrude Lawrence as well. The newest plaque is one to the memory of Otis Skinner's famous daughter, Cornelia Otis Skinner, who died in 1979. But because of its early acceptance of social and economic outcasts, this actors' church has become equally famous for its appeal to young lovers; couples come from all over the country to be married there. The imposing church still stands on a corner of Madison Avenue, cold as ever. And on the coldest of Holy Thursdays, the Little

Church Around the Corner was still the warmest place in town.

And while we're on the subject of weather, I have advice for tourists coming to the States this summer, whether you're coming to sticky-hot New York, or going to Florida which is even hotter. I went down to Tampa, Florida a few weeks ago to take part in a symposium at the University of South Florida, and I was looking forward to a few days in the warm Florida sun. And it was, indeed, warm and sunny as I walked across the green, tree-shaded lawns that frame the college buildings. But the buildings, built twenty-five years ago in the severe white modern architecture of the fifties, looked cold and forbidding and I realized this was because they had very few windows. Some buildings had no windows at all. Which should have warned me. I stepped out of the warm sun into a college building and nearly froze to death. What few windows the building had were sealed shut. The entire university is air-conditioned, cold and clammy, all year round. We came out into the sun at lunchtime and walked to a nearby restaurant, and the restaurant was also cold and clammy, whereupon the professor who escorted me told me that the entire state of Florida is air-conditioned to pneumonia-levels all year round.

Well, I have to warn you that in summer, the same thing is true of New York. Whether we're going to the supermarket or to a concert at Lincoln Center, all of us take sweaters with us, especially on very hot days and evenings. So if you're coming to my town this summer, bring your thinnest summer dresses and your warmest sweaters.

Which reminds me of the first joke I ever heard about English weather, back in the days when I was a schoolgirl. It seems a young lady was planning her first visit to London and wrote to an English dowager to ask what clothes she would need.

"When coming to London," the dowager wrote back, "bring a fur coat, an organdy dress, and an umbrella."

MAY

We've had such marvelous May weather that one sign of summer has set in a month early. On a summer Sunday the avenues are so empty you think all of New York has gone to the beach or the country. Maybe a third of the population has left town. The other two thirds have gone to Central Park for the day. Among all the world's parks, I suspect Central Park is unique—a big word which I'll try to justify.

Since Manhattan Island is a narrow strip, twelve miles long by less than two miles wide at its widest, the first singular fact about Central Park is that its 840 acres sit smack in the middle of the scarcest, most expensive and overcrowded real estate in the world. It runs north through town from 59th Street to 110th, its eastern boundary is Fifth Avenue, its western boundary is a few blocks from Broadway.

It's entirely man-made. Frederick Law Olmsted, the genius who created it, had to import, place, plant and build every inch of a landscape twice the size of the principality of Monaco. He built it on half a dozen levels. There are not only hills and valleys and high rocky cliffs above rowboat lakes, there's a model sailboat pond below street level; and Belvedere Plaza, so deep underground it's reached only by two long flights of steps downward. So there are stone foot bridges and underpasses everywhere, as well as dirt paths leading to woodlands. One woodland called the Ramble, full of winding paths and small streams, is so hushed on a summer day, it's impossible to believe you're standing within half a mile of Fifth Avenue on one side and Broadway on the other.

But its real uniqueness lies in the fact that Central Park is *not* for New Yorkers to look at and admire, but to use, as an estate which belongs to them. Olmsted gave it to us, and successive generations of benefactors keep adding to the gift. We ourselves add to it when we can, as befits owners. This is what the estate contains:

There are miles of bridle paths, bike roads, jogging paths. There are rowboat lakes for family outings, stocked with fish for boys in rolled-up jeans to fish for. There's a swan lake, with benches around it so old men can play chess there. There's a stone-rimmed pond for model sailboat owners, and ponds with grassy banks where toddlers can make mud pies while their dogs go swimming. There are ice-skating and roller-skating rinks, baseball diamonds and tennis courts, basketball and shuffleboard courts. There are lawns so vast that there's room for a quarter of a million people to sit on the grass, on a summer night, for Philharmonic concerts and Metropolitan Opera performances, and pop concerts by Barbra Streisand and Simon and Garfunkel. There are rock-and-roll dances on summer nights down at the 59th Street skating rink, and a Harlem dance group performs up at the other end of the park. There's a bandshell seating several hundred at band concerts on the Mall at East 72nd Street; there's the Shakespeare Theatre on a hill at West 81st Street, built by donations from all of us, with seats for three thousand people but room for several hundred more who perch in trees or on overhanging rocks. And all this entertainment is free, paid for by foundations and corporations and millionaire philanthropists.

There are picnic lawns and folk dancing lawns; there are bird walks through the Ramble, led by Park rangers; there are flower walks from the Conservatory Garden, and special flower stories for children.

There's a children's zoo adjoining the adult zoo; there are

children's pony rides, and a carousel, and two marionette theatres. At my park entrance—East 72nd Street—there's a story hour every Saturday at the seated statue of Hans Christian Andersen, who always has a child sitting on his broad bronze knee reading the story of the Ugly Duckling from the open bronze book in his hand. And there's the Alice In Wonderland statuary, a Mad Tea Party with larger-than-life bronze guests—Alice, the Mad Hatter, the March Hare, the Dormouse and the Cheshire Cat. Older children climb up to sit on Alice's head, while small fry stagger in and out among the giant bronze mushrooms under the tea table. Over on the west side of the park there's a mile-long Adventure Trail for teenagers. And at every fourth block the length of the park on the east (or Fifth Avenue) side, there's a preschoolers' playground with sandbox, swings and a picnic table.

I said that the park belongs to us. I've come upon several weddings there over the years. And I know one Central Park booster whose friends gave her a ninetieth birthday supper party in the Central Park Boathouse cafeteria. Even so, the notice I read in last Sunday's *New York Times* was special. It was an obituary notice, the last line of which read: "Memorial service, Monday, May 17, 5 p.m. In the Ramble, in Central Park."

JUNE

All New Yorkers seem to be living out of doors these hot summer days. Walking home up Fifth Avenue I ran into young activists out doing their thing. I signed one petition to Save the Seals and another demanding the government stop selling computer technology to South Africa. And in front of

St. Thomas's church, a young man was sketching a pretty female, surrounded by a crowd of amateur critics waiting to judge his finished work.

When I got home at six, I joined the step sitters to watch the action. We have a lot of young families in the building this year, and the toddler set was out, waiting for Daddy to come home. Max, who is three, had just got his first tricycle and was having trouble with it. He hadn't got the hang of working one pedal with his left foot. When he couldn't get the thing to move using only his right foot, he got off, pushed the tricycle a few steps, then got back on and tried to move it with his right foot again.

The dog owners had already come home and the dogs were out. Toto, the black scottie, was visiting from up the block, and Carol, his mother informed me belligerently:

"New York dogs are the happiest in the world! They're not tied up alone in a yard and forgotten, like dogs in the country! They have a genuine social life!"

Toto's genuine social life had hit a snag at the moment. He was after Ivory, our resident white toy poodle, who was in heat. But Bentley, the Old English sheepdog, had backed Ivory into a cave under my knees and was trying to tunnel through to her, so every time Toto tried to get at her he came up against a solid wall of sheepdog. Then my friend Nina came home from the supermarket and said to me as she went by:

"Come up on Sunday morning and see my terrace."

Nina's terrace is twenty feet long by five feet wide. When I went up there on Sunday I found on the narrow cement strip two orange trees and one apple tree, (the other one died last year), a lime tree, eighteen flower boxes and sixty-three flower pots. Full of ageratum, anemones, cleones, geraniums, larkspur, marigolds, pansies, petunias, snapdragons, sweet peas and zinnias. Not forgetting a yellow flower called "Poached Egg," another called "Candy Tuft," and pink climber roses flourishing on the back wall. And when I admired everything, all Nina said was:

"Have you seen Monroe's terrace?"

"Who's Monroe?" I asked.

"My neighbor!" said Nina. And she pointed across the open space between our apartment house and the one next door, to a terrace separated from hers only by a few feet—and by a sheer drop to the street, a hundred and fifty feet below—and said: "You have to see it. I'm sure he's out there, he's probably around on the other side." So we took the elevator down sixteen flights, walked next door, took an elevator up sixteen flights and found Monroe round at the side on his terrace. It's a big one; it turns two corners.

Monroe has a rowan tree in an enormous tub, and he told me that cuttings from it were growing in friends' suburban lawns in Connecticut, Long Island and New Jersey. And I want you to know I've been invited to go berry-picking on Monroe's terrace in a few weeks. He has a mulberry tree, strawberry plants, raspberry and blueberry bushes, and they yield more berries than he can use.

"Last June," he said, "I had so many mulberries I froze half of them and ate them at Christmas time."

But the big attraction for all three of us was Monroe's mockingbird, roosting twenty yards above his terrace, high up on the water tower—a stone drum perched on iron pipes that supplies water to the building. And since Monroe said the bird is found only in the U.S., I looked it up for you. A mockingbird—officially a mimic thrush—can, and does, imitate the songs of thirty birds. Well, Monroe was away one week and when he came home, his next-door neighbor said: "You have a blue jay on your terrace, I hear him every morning!" And the terrace-owner above him called down, "There's a crow around here somewhere, have you heard him?" And a woman up the hall met him at the elevator and said: "Do you have a canary?" So Monroe, who grew up around mockingbirds, knew what bird to look for. They're grey with white undersides.

Monroe's so pleased to have one, that I don't like to tell him *why* the mockingbird is roosting on the water tower above his terrace. According to my encyclopedia, while mockingbirds live mainly on insects, their favorite food is fruit—especially berries.

AUGUST

Next week I'm flying to London, and considering how many times I've done it, you'd think I could just get on a plane and go. But I'll be gone a month, and you won't believe what I'm going through in preparation for the trip.

In the first place, I am being persecuted by British Airways. I won't fly at night because you get to London at four a.m. American time and walk around like a zombie with jet lag for two days. So I'm taking BA's dear little day flight. I love to sit by the window and look out at the sky and the clouds below, and the ocean. To do this, you have to sit far back in the smoking section, where they don't make you pull down the window blind to watch some miserable movie when you'd rather look at the universe. Since I smoke, this works out fine, and when I bought my ticket I asked BA to reserve me a window seat far back in the smoking section. They wouldn't do it. They said I have to wait till I get to the airport and ask for it there—and you *know* all the window seats will be gone by then. So if the president of BA is a close friend of yours, call him and tell him he's ruining my trip.

Two days after I lost the argument with BA, I was persecuted by the luggage department of Alexander's Department Store. Last fall when I went to London for a week, I borrowed my neighbor Dimitria's pale powder-blue suitcase and, at the Heathrow luggage wheel that suitcase positively shouted its location to me, standing out in a sea of dark brown, dark red and dark plaid luggage. Since Dimitria had bought it at Alexander's, I went down there to buy the largest powder-blue suitcase they had, so it would hold everything. One suitcase is enough to annoy yourself with.

Now Alexander's is a very cheap department store, with a do-it-yourself luggage department. I picked out a mammoth powder-blue suitcase, dragged it to the checkout table, heaved it up onto the counter and handed the lady my credit card. She rang up the sale and then stuck signs all over the suitcase saying I'd paid for it, so the store detective wouldn't shoot me when I walked out with it. Then she pushed it back to me. No wrapping paper, no shopping bag big enough to hold it, and at these prices Alexander's wasn't about to mail it to me.

I lugged it down four escalator flights and out onto Third Avenue, where a bus pulled up and stopped right in front of me. And at the five p.m. rush hour, in my right mind, I got on the bus. *We* got on the bus. Standing room only, and from then on, people boarding the bus tripped over me and my suitcase. We took up the whole aisle.

Arlene came to dinner, to inspect my wardrobe for the trip. She made me take all my clothes out of the closet and hold up every jacket and pair of pants and told me which blouse and sweater to wear with which pants. Everything was the wrong texture for everything else. She made me separate the clothes into piles—one pile for cold weather, one for heat waves, one for around-the-house, and a pile to be sent to Goodwill Industries for distribution to the poor.

Since I'm taking a day flight, she made a list of the

emergency food I'm to take with me, because when I go to
bed in London at midnight, it'll only be seven p.m. my time
and I may wake up at three a.m. starved. André Deutsch, my
publisher, is giving me the top floor of his house for my stay
in London, but Arlene pointed out I could *not* sneak down
two flights of stairs in my nightgown at three in the morning,
to raid André's kitchen. So I'm to take a tin of powdered milk,
a jar of peanut butter and two hard-boiled eggs.

Then she cut my hair (all over the carpet) because she
didn't like the way the hairdresser had cut it, and criticized my
comb because a few teeth were missing. I don't use a comb (I
use a brush). Then she asked what makeup I was taking. "I'm
too old for makeup," I said. "I have a lipstick." "I've seen it,"
said Arlene. She stepped back and glared down at me.

"When I travel," she said, "I take a leather hatbox packed
with cosmetics. *You* take a comb with no teeth and the stub
end of a lipstick you won't give up because you like the color
and they don't make it anymore. Which doesn't surprise me,
you must've bought it in 1965!"

She inspected the BA flight bag I'm packing for weekend
trips and told me it wasn't big enough. Then she gave me a big
kiss, said she'd had a super evening and went home. The next
morning a package arrived with an enormous red, white and
blue striped cotton shopping bag, for weekend trips. Pinned
to it was a note: "Don't carry it! Wear it slung over your
shoulder."

OCTOBER

I first met my friend Bernadette six years ago when she was
senior editor of a magazine—and meeting her was like saying
hello to an elf. She's five feet tall, she weighs ninety pounds—

six stone plus—she has short dark hair like a cap, a pert face and a friendly, toothy smile. We discovered we were both music-lovers and we began going to Lincoln Center concerts together. And, at one October concert I said I was going to get on a bus the next Sunday and ride up to Bear Mountain to see the autumn foliage. Bernadette looked worried.

"You won't see any trees from a bus!" she said. "Buses take the highways!"

That Friday night she phoned me. "My brother-in-law is going to drive us to Bear Mountain Sunday to see the leaves," she said. "He knows that area, he'll take the country roads."

We went, and I had a wonderful time. Bern was happy, too, but I suspected she'd have been just as happy staying home with the Sunday *Times*.

At a concert the following spring, I learned that her former secretary, the secretary's mother *and* their dog had moved into the living room of Bern's one-bedroom apartment. "I ran into them on the street," she said. "They can't find an apartment and they had nowhere to go!"

They stayed for weeks, running up Bern's phone bill and food bill. Not till they suggested she give them her bedroom and sleep on the living room sofa-bed herself, did Bern get hard-hearted enough to throw them out. Every deadbeat in town goes to Bernadette for free dinners and loans that are never paid back.

"You let people take advantage of you!" I said. She's not naive or gullible and I couldn't understand it.

I also had trouble adjusting to her hobby which is reading palms and Tarot cards. She's always reporting that she *told* her doorman he was going to get a promotion and he's just been made superintendent, or she saw marriage in her art director's Tarot cards, and the art director just called to invite her to the wedding.

But she has far more depth and talent than any of this

suggests. Last summer, she answered one of those half-page ads in the Sunday *Times* that companies run when they're looking for a high-powered executive. She was called for an interview and afterward learned that there'd been three hundred applicants for the job, the field had been narrowed to thirty and she was one of the thirty. When the field narrowed to three, she was one of the three. Then one day she phoned in wild excitement to tell me she'd got the job. At thirty-seven she had become director of a large publishers' association.

But when the president of the company briefed her, she was very apprehensive. He told her she was the first woman executive the company'd ever hired and that some of the men working with her, and the men working under her, would probably resent her. A week went by before she phoned to report, with awe, that every man in the place was going out of his way to help her.

"I can't understand it!" she said. I could. I'd learned the key to her by then. I learned it one night when we met at a new restaurant for dinner before a concert. As usual, Bern ordered a white wine aperitif, I ordered a martini.

"We don't have martinis," said the waiter. "We only serve wine."

Bern stared at him, aghast. Then she was on her feet.

"We'll be right back," she told the waiter. "Come on," she said to me and streaked out the front door. I followed her down the street to a bar-and-grill, where Bernadette went up to the bar and said to the bartender:

"We'd like a martini to take out."

The bartender stared down at his pint-sized customer with his mouth open.

"In twelve years of tending bar," he said, "I never had *anybody* order a martini-to-go."

But he made the martini, poured it into a plastic glass and

handed it to Bernadette. I paid him and then had to run after Bern who was carrying the martini up the street and into the restaurant. I reached her as she was setting the glass down at my place. She slid into her seat opposite, gave me a pleased smile and said:

"I wanted you to be happy."

Bernadette goes through life trying to make the entire world happy.

NOVEMBER

I have got the most aggravating dog story for you. It's about Tara, the female Doberman pinscher who lives in the liquor store—the off-license—across the street. Several years ago, when Bill and his wife became owners of the liquor store, they bought Tara to guard it. She was three months old when she arrived, an affable pup staggering around on pelican-long legs, and the whole neighborhood paraded into the store to see her.

Nobody told Tara she was a watchdog and she grew up docile and amiable; I've never heard her bark, much less growl. She's a bit standoffish till she knows you. But once you're her friend, if you bring her a toy she leaps up, puts both front paws on your shoulders, nearly knocking you down, and licks your face so enthusiastically your sunglasses go flying off into the vin rosé.

But of course burglars don't know this. Tara is alone in the store from ten p.m. to ten a.m., and no burglar, looking through the lighted picture window at the huge sleeping Doberman lying just inside the front door, has ever felt inclined to disturb her.

During the day, Tara is a neighborhood landmark. Since there are no other windows in the store, Bill and his wife usually keep the front door open and Tara's favorite pastime is standing out on the sidewalk by herself, watching the steady stream of people and dogs, cars and buses go by. She never ventures into the street or up the block. 72nd Street is a busy thoroughfare and Tara's happy, standing stock-still on the sidewalk, surveying the world.

Now and then some terrified stranger will detour into the gutter to avoid her and then phone the police to report a vicious Doberman pinscher standing on the sidewalk with no leash and no supervision, menacing the neighborhood and the police will phone Bill, and he'll keep Tara indoors for a day or two till it blows over. When this happens, our whole street is up in arms: Tara should be allowed out in the sun!

Now even though Bill had to install a padlocked iron gate in front of the door at night, to satisfy his insurance company, Tara is left alone there every weekend from Saturday till Monday morning, except for ten-minute visits by somebody who's paid to feed her and walk her on Sundays, since Bill and his wife live in the suburbs. But what really upsets us are the long holiday weekends when Tara is shut up alone in the closed store from Saturday night till Tuesday morning, and we always stop and say hello to her when we see her peering out of her picture window at the world going by.

Well, last month we had our first long holiday weekend of the season. And that weekend, whenever I glanced across the street at the forbidding iron gate that encloses both door and picture window, and thought of Tara alone behind it, I got depressed. That Tuesday morning I went into the store with a soup bone which my friend Nina had saved for Tara. But Tara wasn't there. Neither was Bill's wife.

"Where's my friend?" I asked Bill. He got expansive.

"We took her home with us for the weekend," he said. "But my wife had to wait home today for some furniture, and I didn't want to drive in alone with Tara, she's not used to cars, so I gave her an extra day off."

I came out of there so happy I floated home. Tara was finally a member of the family, going home for long holiday weekends with her folks. When I took her her soup bone the next morning, I said:

"Did you have a good time on your holiday, hon?"

"No, she didn't," said Bill's wife. "She was homesick."

She was what?

"She was homesick for the liquor store," said Bill's wife. "She wandered around the house like a lost soul. Yesterday, she refused to go out. I had to drag her to the curb."

I told this to Nina when she came by the next morning, and she laughed. "Tara's the president of 72nd Street," she said. "She missed the action! Even in the store, there's action, people coming and going all day. What would she do in the suburbs?"

Nina had come down that morning to bring me a large red apple tied with a green bow, because the apple came from her own apple tree. Nina bought a dwarf apple tree six years ago, a pitiful, scrawny thing that shivered in its pot on her sixteenth-floor terrace. It's now a genuine shade tree, with—at last count—twenty-four perfect apples on it.

I keep feeling there's a connection somewhere—between a New York dog homesick for a liquor store and an apple tree, flourishing on a narrow strip of cement, sixteen stories above the ground—but I can't find it. Maybe it's that both dogs and trees adapt to New York's life-style. And maybe it's just that things happen in this town that wouldn't dream of happening anywhere else.

DECEMBER

Two weeks ago, when *84, Charing Cross Road* opened on Broadway, two special Londoners were in the audience. The play is about my correspondence with a London bookseller named Frank Doel, and though he and his wife are both dead now, their two daughters wrote to tell me they were planning a once-in-a-lifetime trip to New York to attend the opening.

Carried away by this news, I sent out elegant invitations to eighteen friends, to meet Sheila Doel Wheeler and Mary Doel Childs at a buffet supper in my one-and-a-half-room apartment. I knew that seating and serving everybody would be no problem. My long modern sofa seats eight or ten, and there's a long coffee table in front of it and end tables flanking it, for setting dinner plates down. On the other side of the living room there's an armchair and a Swedish rocker, both with end tables—and what with dinette chairs and my plush new wall-to-wall carpet to curl up on, I knew I wouldn't have to use the alcove—a half room just big enough for my bookshelves, desk and typewriter table—which I like to keep dark during a party.

The problem was how to cook supper for twenty in my doll's house kitchen. The menu included hot Mexican chili, cold turkey, hot corn bread and raw vegetable salad, followed by homemade brownies and homemade sour cream coffee cake. New Yorkers are used to managing this in a kitchen five feet wide by seven feet long, with one small counter to work on and a small refrigerator, but it requires ingenuity and cooperative neighbors.

A week before the party, I made the corn bread, the brownies and the coffee cake and took them all up to 16-B and put them in Nina's freezer. (Nina lives in a penthouse. Penthouses have large freezers.) Since my biggest stewpot holds only enough chili for eight or ten, I borrowed Nina's biggest stewpot and made chili in both. I made it several days in advance and then packed the chili into the eight one-pound coffee tins my friend Arlene and I had collected. I put four of the tins in my freezer and carried the other four up the hall to 8-E and put them in Susan and Alan's freezer. This left half my freezer for ice. Americans like lots of ice in their drinks, and I made enough by emptying two ice trays into plastic bags twice a day for four days and asking Dimitria, across the hall in 8-I, to do the same.

On Saturday, the day of the party, I got my baked goods back from 16-B and my chili from 8-E, and while they were thawing out, I put both leaves in my dinette table and covered it with my best linen cloth. Then, since I don't own twenty of anything, I set the table with my silverware and Nina's, and my white china and her white china, with Arlene's opulent silver chafing dish for the chili, and her enormous, two-inch-deep fish platter for the raw vegetable salad, with Nina's fifty-cup, banquet-sized coffee pot waiting to be plugged in, in the kitchen.

Then I went down to the lobby and asked Danny, our super, to send up the coatrack the building keeps for tenants' parties. It's a long, horizontal steel pole between two upright steel poles, and I parked it in the hall outside my front door for the evening.

The party was a roaring success, but, of course, while I was serving cake and coffee, four busybody female guests decided to do the dishes. Now Susan and Alan in 8-E had been told I'd need their dishwasher. They had *not* been told that four strange women, carrying armloads of dirty dishes, would be parading into 8-E while its occupants were having a late supper in their bathrobes.

On Sunday morning, rising early to clean up the mess, I went out to the kitchen, planning to put my stewpot to soak before breakfast. Nina's stewpot was sitting on the counter, clean. My stewpot had disappeared. It wasn't in the fridge, it wasn't in the oven, it wasn't in the pots and pans cabinet. So when various guests phoned to say it was a great party, I said: "Thank you, do you know where my stewpot is?" Nobody knew till my friend Maxine, the actress, phoned. She and her husband had flown in from Hollywood for the opening, and had attended the party.

"Your stewpot's in 8-E," said Maxine. "We carried the silverware and cups and saucers down the hall in it, it was our last load."

When I finished cleaning, I let myself into 8-E to get everything out of the dishwasher, and I was glad Susan and Alan had gone to a wedding and weren't home. My iron stewpot was sitting on their kitchen counter, shining clean. *They* must have scoured it—in their bathrobes—before they went to bed.

NINETEEN EIGHTY-THREE

1983

JANUARY

First, a couple of Christmas items I didn't get round to last month. I don't remember when Arlene started giving me twelve Christmas presents, one for each of the twelve days of Christmas, but she's been doing it for years. (We fight about this every year; I always lose.) A few are expensive, all twelve are useful but they always include three or four so far out they have to be explained to me. Herewith, this year's collection:

The expensive items were two sets of Bloomingdale's chic-est place mats and napkins, my favorite bath powder, and a beautiful silk scarf. Next came a set of wooden napkin rings, an apron with caricatures of Broadway stars on it, an angora beret, and—because I like Chinese takeout food—a dozen chopsticks. That left four What-Is-Its. Two were plates, one with hollowed-out ovals, the other with hollowed-out rounds and I had to be told that the first was for deviled eggs and the second for artichokes. Add a metal stamp reading good morning in mirror printing, which you stamp on your bread before you toast it so your morning toast will say "good morning" to you. And we come to Number 12, the What-Is-It of all time. Number 12 was two bright-red terry cloth mitts, each the size of a football, the two joined by a length of rope. First you wash your hair. Then you sling the rope around your neck, slip your hands into the enormous mitts and dry your hair with them.

And a Christmas note on this year's wildest gift for the person-who-has-everything. It was one of those electric bicycles you pedal away on, in your living room, to lose weight, but this one came with a video screen. As you rode your bike, the scenery of Southern California went by on your video screen, and soon you were biking through Beverly Hills. After Southern California, you took a short bike tour of the moon. And all for only twenty thousand dollars.

Which brings me to my own recent persecution by the electronic age. All my life I've used a standard manual typewriter. It's a Royal, and when one of the keys broke last week, I phoned the Royal repairman as usual. But this time, when he came, he looked at the broken key and said:

"I can't fix this for you. Royal stopped making standard manuals, they only make electric typewriters now. And since they don't make manuals, they don't carry spare parts for them any more."

I tried an electric typewriter when they first came out thirty years ago. If you paused in your typing to hunt for a word, with your fingers above the keys, the electric typewriter went on typing. So I went back to my manual. But my friend Lolly, who's in the insurance business where you don't hunt for words, switched to an electric some time ago, and told me she had a fine Royal standard to get rid of. Did I want it? So as soon as the repairman left, I phoned her and said, "Yes, I want it."

Now Lolly lives three long crosstown blocks and five short streets from me, but she is always trying to save my money, and she wouldn't hear of the word "taxi." She had a dolly, she said, and she and I could pull the typewriter to my house on it. Early the next morning I hurried to Lolly's apartment house. The dolly wasn't the solid platform-on-wheels that movingmen use. It was homemade, of two long wooden planks with three wooden crossbars nailed to them. But it did have wheels, and after we eased the typewriter onto it, I picked up the lead rope and dragged the contraption behind me to the elevator with no trouble, Lolly bringing up the rear to keep an eye on us.

Once on the sidewalk, however, as I dragged the dolly behind me, I discovered that when I moved to the left to avoid a pedestrian, the wheels of the dolly did NOT move to the left, but the typewriter did. To make things more inter-esting, the middle crossbar fell off.

I am small and thin; Lolly is large and imposing. And as we paraded across York Avenue, a wide thoroughfare—I going one way, the wheels going another and Lolly behind us using the fallen crossbar to hook the typewriter as it slid—we stopped traffic. Early-morning dog walkers and commuters in cars watched, fascinated, as Lolly called instructions to me in her stately voice: "Swerve RIGHT." "Inch slowly LEFT." Later, when the typewriter threatened to fall into the hole left by the missing plank, Lolly called "STOP" and bent and lifted the typewriter out of the hole, though we were in the middle of First Avenue traffic at the time. Never mind. We got the typewriter here safely.

It's a beautiful machine, newer and in far better condition than mine. But I didn't throw mine out. If anything ever breaks on Lolly's and a repairman tells me he can't replace it, I've got a whole typewriter full of spare parts, sitting perma-nently on the closet floor.

FEBRUARY

If you grew up in America in the thirties or forties, no place-name conjured up as much glamour as the name "Hollywood." You read about the studios, about the fabulous homes in Beverly Hills, and about Grauman's Chinese theatre where opulent movie premieres were held and where stars planted their footprints in wet cement to preserve them for posterity. But it was hard to believe that Hollywood was a real place on a map. It seemed a fantasy land, as imaginary as El Dorado.

Well, my oldest friend, Maxine, lives in Los Angeles. And last month I went out to visit her, startling myself by being very excited at the prospect of actually setting foot in the fantasy land of my growing up.

Maxine is an actress married to a TV writer, and they live in Westwood, an attractive college community but not a college town. Because the first thing you discover about the city of Los Angeles, as you drive through it, is that there *is* no city, and there are no surrounding towns. Los Angeles is a vast sprawl of neighborhoods that drift in all directions but have no center and none of the features that mark a city. There's no theatre district, there's no main shopping district. There's no cluster of government buildings, no financial district, no museum area. Most startling of all, there are few solid buildings. Along the thousands of streets are structures that are like shacks, one or two stories high, of wood or stucco and painted in gaudy colors. They look more like roadside stands than buildings, and they seem to have been thrown up haphazardly to house stores selling food or clothes or TV sets or whatever. Here and there we passed a huge new stone apartment house towering above the landscape, in which, Maxine told me, you can buy an eight-room penthouse for only seven million dollars. As we drove through all this, I said,

"I want to see Hollywood," and Maxine said: "This *is* Hollywood."

But eventually we did drive past the great gates of the old MGM studios and then on to the old Selznick studios, where Maxine had to pick up a TV script for an audition. And there in front of me was the original Selznick building—the white clapboard neo-Southern mansion which used to appear on the screen at the beginning of every Selznick film. We parked there and went next door to the former Selznick executive offices, now television offices, and for a moment, walking those halls, the old glamour of Hollywood came alive for me. Maxine picked up her script and then said to me: "Would you like to see Grauman's Chinese?" And we drove to what was once the world's most legendary movie palace.

Sid Grauman's Chinese theatre takes up an entire city block and is grotesque beyond description. It's an enormous red and green wooden Chinese pagoda, with green and gold Chinese dragons on the red roof. In its great cement forecourt, we saw the footprints and handprints of the stars, accompanied by their handwritten messages also preserved in cement: "Good luck, Sid." "Thanks to my good friend Sid Grauman."

The next day we drove through Beverly Hills, along heavily wooded roads. I wanted to walk the hilly streets, but you can get arrested for walking there. If you try it, a cop will loom up and ask whom you're visiting. If you're not visiting someone, he'll escort you out. If you come back, he'll arrest you—on the Beverly Hills theory that if you're not visiting one of the residents, you must be there to rob them. So we drove up one woodland road and down the next, looking at the multi-million-dollar homes, that in *no* way resemble the stately homes of England. The houses—all close to the road and close together—are of white or pink stucco with hot-pink stucco roofs. The super-rich Beverly Hills Hotel is also pink stucco, with a hot-pink stucco roof and drenched in pink floodlights. The grounds of the houses, Maxine said, were at the back, full of patios and swimming pools, also floodlit.

But near the entrance to Beverly Hills, it was legal to park the car and walk along Rodeo Drive, said to be the most expensive shopping street in the world. Along with one- and two-story shops, there's a five-level glass complex with boutiques on every level. The shop windows were full of two-hundred-dollar shirts and five-hundred-dollar sweaters, in what are called "California colors"—lavender and peach and aquamarine. And orange leather pants and a jacket in canteloupe suede and a pale silk raincoat lined in mink. The trees along Rodeo Drive were a row of stubby palm trees with tight globes of leaves at the top and no shade. There's a row of these across the street from Grauman's Chinese, there are rows along half the shack-lined streets of Los Angeles, and wherever they are, they look insanely out of place.

I came home with a bad case of Culture Shock and a sense that I ought to have known—not that Hollywood must have changed greatly in four decades, but that it wouldn't have changed at all. Hollywood forty years ago was just what it is now: a town without taste, or grace, or form, or substance. Hollywood was never a glamorous place on the map, it was a glamorous image in the mind, a fantasy land as imaginary as El Dorado. It still is.

What Gertrude Stein said of it fifty years ago is still true: "There isn't any *there* there."

MARCH

You heard about our February blizzard, of course, but all you heard was the one-sided report of the news media, and our news media is absolutely paranoid about snow. Every time a news man predicts snow on the TV evening news, his voice drips with Catastrophe as he exhorts everybody not to go out and not to come into town. This is because all TV newsmen are commuters, live in the suburbs and panic at the thought of snow. They'll have to dig out the driveway, and the car won't start, and the commuter train tracks will freeze and the trains won't be running.

Herewith a city-dweller's report. For New Yorkers, the February blizzard was definitely the high point of the social season. It came on a Friday, which was perfect timing. First, everybody got the afternoon off, since all offices closed early for the commuters. Second, Dad got to go to the park with the kids and their sleds on Saturday and Sunday.

Richard, Bentley the sheepdog, Nina and I went to Central Park at high noon on Saturday, and the plateau at our entrance was as crowded as the winter Olympics, and a lot more festive. The Olympic event was for juniors: it was sledding down hill to the Model Sailboat Pond. The very small fry were on new-style sleds—round red or green plastic dishes; the ten-year-olds were on standard wooden sleds. We only caught glimpses of them, through the dense crowd of onlookers but we wanted to walk anyway. At the far end of the plateau we started downhill through foot-high snow. The road alongside it was cleared, but what city-dweller wants to walk on a cleared path when you can slosh through deep snow? We plowed on toward Dog Hill, Bentley collecting a crowd as he went. Bentley loves snow, but the drifts were high enough to bury him, and he had a special technique for surmounting them. What he did was, he hopped over the snow like a vast, furry rabbit, his huge bulk curving high in midair, his four stubby feet landing lightly and then leaping onward.

We passed other dogs on the way—small ones in their good

winter coats, big ones rolling in the snow with ecstasy—but Dog Hill itself had been taken over by teenagers. They, too, were sledding—but not on sleds. It seems you can sled on anything that's made of plastic. The teenagers were sledding down Dog Hill on plastic trash can lids and plastic raincoats, and two boys, lying one on top of the other, went belly-flopping downhill on a plastic Bloomingdale's shopping bag. When they came back up, Nina borrowed the shopping bag, sat down on it and told Richard to give her a push. He did, and she sailed down the hill in fine style and then came back up and reported: "It's a great ride, but you can't steer!" At which moment a giant plastic trash can lid went zooming downhill past us with a boy in front and his Irish setter behind him, both sitting bolt upright. You can't steer a trash can lid either, and they narrowly missed a tree.

Sunday was different. My friend Bernadette and I went to an afternoon concert at Lincoln Center, which is across town on the West Side, and after the concert, we walked home across the park. At five-thirty on Sunday afternoon, the atmosphere was transformed. The crowds were gone, the park was hushed, and in the pink twilight the snow was luminous, the white landscape framed by the skyline, where pinpoints of light were coming on in high-rise apartment houses. We passed a few solitary walkers and a straggle of cross-country skiiers going by on the main road; and a lone brown dachshund came along, off leash and very natty in a green turtleneck sweater, walking importantly by himself, ten yards ahead of his folks.

I never see a dog dressed for snow without remembering Chester, Richard's first sheepdog. It's the practice in our neighborhood for the doorman of each building, after shoveling the sidewalks, to sprinkle chemical salt on the remaining snow to melt it before it turns icy. But chemical salt can burn a dog's feet. So the day after a snowstorm, people going past our building used to stop dead at the sight of Chester, a huge Old English sheepdog, wearing four red ankle boots.

This year I noticed there was much less of the chemical stuff on the streets. Coming home from the park that Sunday with Bernadette, I saw a Park Avenue doorman sprinkling his sidewalk from a box of ordinary table salt. I asked him why he wasn't using the chemical salt. And I'm sure he meant to say "owners," but what he *said* was:

"The dogs complained about it."

Why not? They're tenants, too.

APRIL

My friend Arlene is currently working as consultant to some New York State Democrats, her friend Mickey is a police chief, and they both work down in the government district of Lower Manhattan. One day a few weeks ago, Arlene phoned me on her lunch hour.

"How much brown wrapping paper can you use?" she asked. I said I didn't need any. "It's only ten cents for a huge roll!" she said. "Each roll's three feet long, it's got yards of paper on it, I could get you a lifetime supply for a dollar!"

I live in a one-room apartment with two closets.

"Where," I asked her, "would I put ten huge rolls of wrapping paper each three feet long?"

Arlene sighed.

"You're right," she said, and bought me one roll for a dime. But a few days later I had dinner with her and Mickey and learned the story behind the wrapping paper. It seems there's a store down in the government district which becomes an addiction to people who work in the area. They wander innocently into it one day on their lunch hour and become hooked. The store apparently buys out the supplies of bankrupt businesses and discontinued product lines and puts the stock on sale at prices nobody can resist and its hapless customers find themselves buying job-lots of things they don't need.

"You go in there," said Mickey, "and they've got seven hundred and fifty-eight feet of rope on sale for thirty-five cents. And you buy it and cart it home and what are you gonna do with seven hundred and fifty-eight feet of rope in a New York apartment?" He said a cop came into his office with a sack of nails and said, "Look what I bought for a buck!"

"So," said Mickey, "he's got twenty-seven pounds of nails in his garage in Brooklyn. Rusting."

And he told me about the elevator operator who got on the subway with a 60-pound bag of fertilizer he was lugging out to Queens, to use on his pocket-size front lawn.

There are also bargains for women. Fine china plate at one third the retail price, brand name lipsticks for a nickel each, and Arlene's latest find—a bar of soap for twenty-seven cents that sells in our local health food store for two dollars. And of course at that price, you don't buy a bar of soap, you buy a case of it. Because when you come on such a bargain, you can't go home and think it over before buying. Arlene went in one day and saw half a floor of miniature hand-crafted furniture—miniature rocking chairs, end tables, cabinets, each selling for pennies. That night she phoned a friend of hers who collects miniatures. The friend hurried down to the store early the next morning, and the miniatures were gone, replaced by vanity bottles, mirrors and trays for the dressing table women don't use any more. Whether it's bought by store owners or bargain addicts, every job lot is gone the next day.

If you go in every day, sooner or later you'll find truly awesome bargains—in camera equipment, stereo components or matched luggage. But by that time you've discovered your daily trips have cost you a small fortune in bargains you'll never use, and, like Mickey and Arlene, you make a solemn vow to limit yourself to one trip to the store per week thereafter.

It all puts me in mind of my sister-in-law Jane's prize job lot bargain. Years ago, when her children were young and the family had a big house on Long Island, I went out there one Christmas Eve and saw, in the stairwell next to the gleaming white staircase, two hundred rolls of pink toilet paper stacked several feet high. Jane told me proudly she'd bought it at a close-out sale for half price. But she declined my offer to help her carry it upstairs.

"Every time any of us goes upstairs, we'll take a few rolls with us," she said. "That way it won't be a chore to get it up there."

Fine. Only, when I went back out to their house the next Christmas, there were still a hundred rolls of toilet paper stacked in the stairwell. The family had got bored with carrying them upstairs or forgot to carry them up, and they'd become part of the foyer decor.

My mother was staying out there for the holidays that year, and she told me later the situation got so on her nerves she spent the whole holiday week carrying toilet paper upstairs on tiptoe when nobody was looking.

JULY

You know that Prince Charles and Princess Diana went to Newfoundland recently, to help celebrate its two hundred anniversary. But I bet you don't know why Newfoundland was settled in 1783 or where the settlers came from. They came from the City of New York.

It all began on July 4, 1776. That was the day on which England's American colonies declared their independence. But it was also the day on which a British fleet landed in New York harbor, with troops that invaded New York City, conquered it and occupied it. Of the twenty-two thousand inhabitants, twenty thousand had already fled upstate, or to New Jersey or Connecticut which were in Rebel hands, and there were only two thousand people—the sick, the old and the Loyalists—here when the British landed.

But New York was to be an occupied city, and the British capital in America, for the next seven years, during which twenty thousand newcomers arrived here—Tory Loyalists who traveled to New York from all the colonies controlled by the Rebels. Many were rich and came by ship with all their belongings and plenty of money. Some were poor and walked here from their native colonies, arriving exhausted and destitute, just to live under the Crown. By which time New York, the Loyalist capital, was also becoming known as "the city of prisons."

There was only one proper prison, but there were many Protestant churches, despised by the Church of England. Thousands of American prisoners of war were thrown into these churches, which became de facto prisons. But to the British Army, these were not prisoners of war; they were British subjects who had committed high treason.

In one church prison that first summer men died of thirst, one block from the city pump, because nobody bothered to bring them water. When winter came, church prisoners broke up the pews for firewood. By the third winter there were no pews to burn, and men died of trichinosis from eating the raw, wormy pork which was their chief ration. More died of wounds that went untreated.

Rebel sailors captured in battle were put aboard two prison ships in the harbor, one of which was known as the HMS

"Hell," because at night prisoners were stowed down in the hold, then the hatches were battened down, and in the morning, the suffocated corpses were thrown overboard, to make room in the hold for more prisoners.

I have to tell you about my favorite spy. She was a Rebel grandmother and she lived in Brooklyn, on a small farm at the water's edge, with an unobstructed view of the Jersey coast. So Grandma began to hang out a line of washing clearly visible to Rebel lookouts in New Jersey. A row of socks hung with toes facing the sea meant that British troops were moving out; socks facing Brooklyn or New York meant fresh British troops arriving. Colored petticoats meant that Hessian mercenaries had landed; white ones meant they'd moved out. And so forth. All went well till the day Grandma had important news to send to Jersey and so far forgot herself as to hang out her washing in the pouring rain. That's when the British tumbled to her and caught her. And hanged her.

Meanwhile, the well-to-do Tories in New York were having a fine time giving charity balls to aid destitute Loyalists, attending glittering receptions for the visiting Prince of Wales, and going to church on Sunday to pray for victory. But at the end of 1781 it was the Rebels who were victorious. The war dragged on another year, but by 1783 it was all over, and the occupation army was to move out in November.

All that summer and fall Loyalists who refused to live under a Rebel government cast about for somewhere to go. Those who could afford it booked passage for London or Edinburgh or Dublin. But many couldn't afford the trip, or the cost of living in a British capital. So His Majesty's government offered them free passage to a far-off wilderness called the New-Found Land. And that fall, these descendants of English settlers became pilgrims and pioneers all over again, settling a northern outpost they named St. John, in Newfoundland. Once more, twenty thousand people left New

York—and the twenty thousand New Yorkers who had fled it seven years earlier came home.

So now you know why New York has huge fireworks displays on the Fourth of July—and why Prince Charles and Princess Diana traveled all the way to Newfoundland, to shake hands with the descendants of one-time New Yorkers.

SEPTEMBER

Since this was the hottest, longest summer in New York history, with a heat wave early in June and the temperature reaching ninety-nine degrees on the eleventh of September, you might expect New Yorkers to spend the summer indoors in their air-conditioned apartments. They didn't. The whole town jumped with out-of-doors action this summer.

Up and down Fifth Avenue and along the side streets, food stands did a thriving business, selling Greek souvlaki, American hot dogs and soda pop and Italian ices, especially at lunch time. Office workers and vacationing students carried their lunches to Rockefeller Plaza or ate them sitting on the stone ledge next to skyscraper reflecting pools, and watched the world go by. After lunch, the office workers had time for a little shopping on Fifth Avenue sidewalks. Peddlers spread out their wares—T-shirts and jeans, handbags, belts and running shoes—on the hot sidewalks in the teeth of and sometimes in front of, air-conditioned Saks Fifth Avenue.

For those with no office hours to keep, there was free outdoor entertainment all over town. The biggest attraction was the Lincoln Center Out-of-Doors Festival, at an open-air theatre around the fountains. Every day, starting at ten a.m. and going on at intervals till eight p.m., there were chamber music and country music groups, ballet companies, dance bands, a black theatre company, a musical-comedy troupe, a puppet theatre, and there was Chinese folk-dancing and a seminar for clowns—and I'm only touching the highlights.

Down in Greenwich Village crowds were drawn by street performers including a tightrope walker, walking a high wire between skyscrapers, and four young men juggling flaming torches, as well as the standard folk singers, guitarists, marimba bands and tap dancers. Down on the Lower East Side and up in Harlem, itinerant acting companies set up makeshift theatres on street corners. And up at Riverside Church modern dance companies gave free performances on the church roof, right under the bell tower.

On Saturday mornings everybody set out for their neighborhood greenmarket. Nina and I set out with our shopping bags early in search of Jersey tomatoes, peaches and damson plums, trying to get to the greenmarket in the 67th Street schoolyard before the mob, but we never did; it was always jammed when we got there.

The dogs also had a great summer, thanks partly to the young professional dog walkers. On my way to the park one afternoon I came to an apartment house with the usual canopy held up by two poles driven into the sidewalk at the curb, and saw, attached to the two poles by their leashes, a total of nine dogs, and I made a note of them for you. There was a Russian wolfhound, a pair of West Highland brothers, a German shepherd, a long-haired dachshund, a shih-tzu, an Airedale, a part-golden retriever and a bearded collie. They were all sitting or lying down, obviously waiting, so *I* waited. A few minutes later a young woman came out of the apartment house with dog No. 10, an Irish setter, who greeted his friends enthusiastically as the young woman unhooked the nine leashes. Then, with five leashes in each hand, she set off calmly with her charges for Central Park, several blocks away. The canine entourage took up the entire sidewalk, but passersby coming toward them just grinned and stepped out into the street to let them pass. I followed the ten tails, the short ones straight up in the air, the long ones waving from side to side, clear to Central Park, where the dog walker headed north for Dog Hill, to let her charges off leash so they could chase sticks and each other and wrestle and roll in the grass for a couple of hours.

As to the rest of Central Park—always the heart of a New Yorker's summer, especially on weekends—I'll let an English tourist tell you about it. Herewith a report from Marilyn Williams of Sutton Coldfield, who was here with her husband, and wrote to me when they got home.

"We thought we'd have a picnic in Central Park and then find Alice in Wonderland," she wrote. "It should have taken us twenty minutes to find her, but because of all the diversions, it took six hours. Never have I seen such happiness! People's faces were lit up. We watched the volleyball, baseball and football games, the roller-skating, the rope-skipping, the jazz bands, the singers, magicians, jugglers. It was all too much! We both agreed it was one of the nicest days we'd ever had."

Blessings on your head, Marilyn.

NOVEMBER

People who live in private houses don't know the meaning of the phrase "community living." There may be a community just outside the front door, but in your own house, especially in the evening, the community is shut out. In a New York apartment house your community lives in the house with you. This has great advantages, especially if you live alone. But it also has chronic aggravations.

Most high-rise apartment houses have thick walls and you

don't hear your next door neighbors. But the ceilings are thin, and the aggravations come from the neighbor overhead. For years I lived under a quiet newspaperman who had a bad habit of falling asleep in front of his TV set in the evening. Our TV goes on all night showing old movies, and I used to be wakened at one a.m. by the shoot-out in some Western overhead. I'd get out of bed, put on a robe and slippers, pad up the back stairs and bang on the newspaperman's door till I woke him up. He was always very apologetic.

The young woman above me now is also quiet. Except on evenings when I've got Bach or Handel on my radio, and she starts practicing scales on her piano. Whereupon I remind myself—counting the toddlers in the building—that at least five tenants recently lived under newborn babies. And more live under dogs who consider it their duty to bark when they hear strange footsteps in their hall. And I remember when the family above Arlene had two small boys who played football on her ceiling.

I live in a rental building where complaints about fellow tenants are made to the super. Arlene's building is a co-op in which the tenants own shares, and they complain to their elected co-op board. My friend Ronnie also lives there and served on the board for a while, and I asked her about complaints.

"Most of them were about dogs," she said. "Every time a dog had an accident in one of the elevators, we heard from tenants who wanted all dogs banned from the house. Then there was the Muzak—canned music—in the elevators. Somebody complained about it to the super, and he took it out. Then somebody complained about his taking it out, and he put it back. Then it came before the board. And you know what Arthur complained about. He's still complaining about it."

I will tell you about Arthur's complaint.

Arlene's and Ronnie's apartment house is huge, with three separate wings. Arlene lives in the A wing, which is very dignified; Ronnie lives in the B wing, which is cheaper and chummier. The C wing, thirty-nine stories high, is known as the Tower and has opulent floor-through penthouses on the top ten floors, occupied by corporate millionaires and millionaire celebrities.

Well, last Fourth of July, our friends Bob and Allie, who live in the B wing, gave a barbecue picnic on the B-wing roof. Ronnie and I were there, and so was Ronnie's neighbor, Arthur Tell. Arthur is an antiques dealer and he's very fussy about the Looks of Things. And halfway through his barbecued chicken, he pointed an accusing finger at a high floor in the Tower, and said to me: "Look at that!"

Strung across the terrace of one of the tower penthouses was a clothesline, hung with wet T-shirts, Bermuda shorts and socks.

"That shouldn't be allowed!" said Arthur. "This is not a tenement! The board should put a stop to it!"

"How," Ronnie asked me, "were we supposed to tell the owners of a million-dollar penthouse they couldn't hang out their wash on their own terrace, if they felt like it?"

Next month, the advantages of community living.

DECEMBER

Okay, I said I'd tell you about the advantages of apartment house living this time; but in five minutes I can give you only a few samples.

I was cooking breakfast one morning at seven-thirty when, on my way from the refrigerator to the frying pan, I dropped the only egg in the house. I went up the hall, listened at the door of 8-E, and hearing movement inside, knocked discreetly. When Alan, young husband of Susan, called, "Who is it?" I said, "Have you got a spare egg?" A moment later the door opened a crack and a bare male arm slid out with an egg at the end of it.

So I was very gratified when, last Monday, there was a knock at *my* door at seven-thirty a.m. and Susan said, "Have you any milk for Alan's coffee? We were skiing this weekend and we forgot to get milk last night when we got home."

Breakfast crises are not the only ones an in-house community solves at inconvenient hours. I wear soft contact lenses. I put them in at seven a.m. and take them out just before midnight. Now and then I drop one, or it flies off my finger for parts unknown and I can't find it. I take two steps across the hall and bang on the door of my eagle-eyed neighbor, Dimitria, who hurries in and finds the lens for me every time, almost supernaturally.

Dimitria is also brightening my dinner menu these winter nights. I live on a restricted diet—no sugar, no starch—and I can't eat a baked potato. My real passion is for baked-potato skins and I can eat them, but I never could bring myself to bake a potato and then throw it out, just to have the skin. No problem; every night at dinner time I bang on Dimitria's door and say, "Your potato's ready!" If she's out to dinner, I take the potato up the hall to Alan. He and Susan get home from work too late to cook them and Susan doesn't eat them anyway; she's always dieting.

Then there was my Saturday laundry crisis. We have coin-operated washers and dryers down in the basement, and one Saturday, after I put my wet wash in the dryer, I inserted my quarters in the slot and pushed—and the slot jammed, halfway in. I couldn't push the slot in far enough to start the dryer, and I couldn't get my quarters out. I rode up to the eighth floor and rang the bell of 8-E, and Alan came to the door on one crutch. He'd sprained his ankle playing tennis. But he insisted on hobbling into the elevator with me and riding down to look at the dryer. He pushed and pushed, but the slot wouldn't budge. "Stand back," he said. Then he stood back. He raised his crutch shoulder-high and—looking like Robin Hood in a jousting tournament—with one great forward blow of his crutch he rammed the slot in, and the dryer started.

Along with crisis solving, there are social advantages to apartment house living. I work at home alone all day, and by five-thirty I may feel the need for company. I go down to the front step where I know that, at least, four-year-old Amanda and five-year-old Max will be waiting with their mothers for Daddy to come home. I went down yesterday and Amanda showed me her new mittens, and Max wanted to know if I'd met Santa Claus yet. He's met him twice—once at F.A.O. Schwarz's Toy Store and once at Bloomingdale's. By six o'clock the dog owners have come home and the dogs come out: Bentley the sheepdog, Adonis the Afghan, Charlie the Cairn, Ivory the white toy poodle, joining Toto and Jeremy, Butch and Cleopatra from up the block.

But, as I'm sure I've told you in past Christmas seasons, next week is the one time in the year when I couldn't manage at all without in-house neighbors. On Christmas Eve my pies will once more be up in 16-B in Nina's freezer, and my sweet potato casserole and homemade cranberry sauce will be down in 4-F North in Richard's refrigerator. He'll bring them up an hour before dinner, when he has to come up anyway, to take the turkey out of the oven for me, because one year I dropped *that*. (I'm small and the turkey wasn't.) When he comes up to Christmas dinner Richard has to bring along his hot tray and his good carving knife. After dinner, he or Arlene's Mickey will wheel my tea cart full of dinner dishes up the hall so I can put them in 8-E's dishwasher since Alan and Susan go to Susan's mother's on Long Island for Christmas.

And a few days before Christmas, Schor the actor, who's home during the day, will set up my Christmas tree for me and string the lights, and Dimitria will make extra ice cubes for me. And if I get nervous on Christmas afternoon about whether the turkey's done or not (I always do), Nina-the-gourmet-cook will come down and look at it for me.

Community living at its finest.

NINETEEN EIGHTY-FOUR

1984

JANUARY

Today we'll consider what New Yorkers are wearing this
season because I have a clothes crisis that's driven everything
else from my mind.

Aside from the Reagan super-rich, who go down the
avenue dripping in mink, every woman in town seems to be
wearing a down coat. Down coats are made of the quilting you
sleep under, they come in all colors, and they remind me of
Bob Cratchit who wore his white comforter to work because
he "boasted no great-coat." Below this comforter the young
especially wear red, blue or lavender leg-warmers over their
jeans or pants. For evening wear, there are black leg-warmers
covered with gold sequins, worn with this year's evening
dresses which seem to be made entirely of gold glitter.

I ignored all this. I'm so small I'd look like a walking coat
hanger in a down quilt and my *chic* friend Arlene helped me
pick out a stunning fake fur coat instead. I live in pants since
the only shoes that fit me are oxfords, which look hideous
with dresses. But my pants are Arlene's designer cast-offs,
they're made of fine wool, so I don't need leg-warmers. And
for rare occasions in my quiet social life requiring evening
wear, I have a black velvet pantsuit of Arlene's for which,

every few years, I buy a new white satin blouse. I've owned the pantsuit since 1975, but since I don't wear it twice a year it still looks new.

Well, just before Christmas, Arlene and her Mickey came to dinner and told me, to my great joy, that they plan to be married at the end of March. I kissed them both, and Mickey said solemnly:

"We have a favor to ask you."

I looked at Arlene.

"We've both been married before, so it's going to be a small wedding," she said. "No bridal procession but Mickey's son is going to be best man, and we want you to be maid of honor."

Arlene is in her glamorous, high-fashion forties. I'm old enough to be her mother and Mickey's grown son's grand-mother. But never having been married myself, I said, pleased:

"I would *love* to be your Old Maid of Honor."

Over the martinis they told me the ceremony is to take place in a private room at Windows on the World, the dazzling restaurant on the hundred-and-seventh floor of the World Trade Center, where dinner will follow for the fifty guests. Arlene also said that just by luck she'd found her wedding dress the previous day. It was a Dior, very simple and Grecian, of grey and white satin. Then she fastened her black eyes on me and said pugnaciously:

"What are *you* going to wear? Not that velvet pantsuit again!"

"It's still beautiful," I said.

"Wear what you want," said Mickey.

"She is not wearing my ten-year-old black velvet pantsuit to my wedding!" said Arlene. "Maids of honor don't wear black!"

"For your wedding, I'm going to buy a proper evening gown," I said.

Arlene looked shocked.

"You're not wearing a dress! I wouldn't know you in a dress!

You'll walk in there in a dress and I'll look at you and think: 'Who's that freak?'"

And finally I said what I'd been expected to say:

"Just tell me what to wear and I'll buy it."

"Get grey satin evening pants," said Arlene. "You can wear your white silk blouse with them." And she added: "I don't know where you're going to find them."

Halfway through dinner, she put down her fork and demanded:

"What are you going to do about your cockamamy feet?!" And she explained to Mickey: "Her heels are so narrow they won't stay in a shoe unless they're laced in! I took her to Gucci's once, just to satisfy myself; I thought their aristocratic customers all had narrow feet and they could fit her. Gucci's wouldn't even let her sit down!" She turned back to me and said: "Go to Capezio's, get white ballet slippers. They're elasticized."

As she left, she remarked that at least I had a great coat and don't worry about the bag, she had a white bag for me.

I have bought the ballet slippers. And I have so far shuffled in and out of the Evening Wear departments of Bergdorf's, Bonwit's and Saks without finding, in the gold glitter, any grey satin pants. I tell myself if I don't find them, I can always resign as Old Maid of Honor—but I don't want to see Arlene's face when I do it.

Tune in for the end of this Suspense Story, if I live to see the end of it.

MARCH

With Arlene's wedding only a week away, you naturally want to know about the social events honoring the happy couple. To understand them you need to know Arlene's history. I told you her profession is running high-powered fund-raising parties, mostly for political candidates. I did not tell you that back in the mid-seventies, one of her clients—Abe Beame— was elected mayor of New York. And he promptly appointed Arlene to the high post of Commissioner for Civic Affairs and Public Events.

The commissioner's duties were to organize official receptions and award ceremonies at City Hall, and run formal luncheons, teas and dinners for visiting dignitaries at Gracie Mansion, the mayor's official residence. But to Arlene, "Public Events" meant huge public parties for seven million New Yorkers. Since the city was bankrupt at the time, she could throw public parties only if they cost the city no money at all.

She went to Ninth Avenue, a mile-long low-income avenue famous for its ethnic food markets, got the owners to agree to set up sidewalk booths for a day and announced the "Ninth Avenue Food Festival." She got Broadway celebrities to mingle with the crowd and serve food at some of the booths and the festival was such a success that it's now an annual New York event, though nobody else knows who started it.

She launched a street fair, called Americana in honor of the Bicentennial to take place on a June Sunday on 52nd Street. She talked so many antique dealers, jewelers, gallery owners and clothing stores into setting up booths that the fair ran along 52nd Street clear across Manhattan Island from the East River to the Hudson. She rounded up folk singers and marimba bands, rock groups and clowns and jugglers to entertain the crowds, free, all along the route. And for weeks before, she commandeered police and sanitation officials to see to it that traffic would be rerouted, crowds patrolled, and the mess cleaned up before Monday morning. (She phoned me one night to say the police department had assigned the *nicest* assistant chief to her project; but she didn't say his name was Mickey, not knowing she would marry him ten years later. And Mickey told me only last week that he was sent to her first meeting, "To talk some crazy broad out of lousing up midtown traffic for an entire Sunday.")

At Christmas Arlene decided New York's slum children needed a party—and she meant slum children from all five cities, called boroughs, now known as "New York." She got bus companies to offer free transportation, she got free lunches from restaurants, free tickets from Radio City Music Hall, free toys from manufacturers. And on five successive days poor children from Manhattan, the South Bronx, Brooklyn, Queens and Staten Island came in to Rockefeller Center for lunch and the Music Hall's Christmas show, followed by a party where every child got a gift from Santa Claus.

During which time she was, of course, running receptions and award ceremonies at City Hall, and a never-ending string of teas and dinners at Gracie Mansion, saving money on them now and then by giving students at New York cooking schools a chance to cater a Gracie Mansion dinner, for the visiting Indian ambassador, or the mayor of Rome or Jerusalem. For four years, she left the house at eight-thirty every morning and got home at midnight. In four years, she took one nine-day vacation. When the four years ended, and Mayor Beame was replaced by Mayor Koch, Arlene declined Koch's invitation to stay on. She was worn out. Memories are short in this fast-moving city. But a few months ago I met a man who now works at City Hall, and when I mentioned Arlene's name, he said simply: "She's a legend down there."

Which explains what happened when news got around that she and Mickey were planning to be married. The chairman of Lincoln Center for the Performing Arts is giving the couple a cocktail party at the Century Club. A Chinese couple—he's a painter, she's a restaurateur—gave a Valentine's Day dinner in their Soho loft for a hundred guests, in honor of the happy couple; the owner of a famous kosher resort hotel gave a St. Patrick's Day shower for Arlene; a fashionable political hostess is giving a large reception for the newlyweds, in her Fifth Avenue skyscraper penthouse on April Fool's Day; and ex-Mayor Beame and his wife are flying up from Florida for the wedding.

Arlene, meanwhile, with a fund-raising dinner to run for New York University, and all the wedding details to see to, had to take a hectic day off last week to shop for a wedding pantsuit for her Old Maid of Honor, the said Maid having failed to find one in five nightmare weeks of shopping.

For the saga of that pantsuit—and the wedding festivities—tune in next month.

APRIL

It was a sad day for me when the Duchess of Windsor retired from public life. The Duchess of Windsor is petite and high-waisted, she has what's called a Junior Miss figure, and when she became the Duchess she wasn't a Junior Miss, she was middle-aged and sophisticated. So fashion designers created chic, simple clothes for her, including evening suits with long sleeves to hide her aging arms. Well, I'm built like the Duchess. Like her I'm a size four, and for years, I bought cheap copies of her clothes in the Junior departments of Fifth Avenue stores.

Then the Duchess retired—and Princess Di came along—and I went shopping for simple grey satin pants to wear to Arlene's wedding as Old Maid of Honor.

Starting at Bonwit's, I went to every store on Fifth Avenue. The Junior departments had debutante ballgowns and short Princess Di evening dresses with ruffles and feathers and little puffed sleeves. The women's departments had evening gowns for the mother-of-the-bride in vast sizes. Nobody had a pair of evening pants, grey satin or otherwise.

I phoned this news to Arlene.

"Forget grey pants, it was a bad idea," she said. "The top of my dress is grey and they might clash."

"If I could see yours . . ." I said.

"No, it's bad luck," said Arlene. "Get a pantsuit in a spring color. Go to the designer departments, they're all having sales, everything's half price."

Designer departments are plush, expensive and intimidating if you're a peasant like me. But starting at Bonwit's again, I went to all of them though my apologetic air and fake-fur coat fairly shouted I didn't belong there. The saleswoman at Bonwit's had no pantsuits to show me; neither did the salesgirls in any other designer department.

I went to the boutiques on Madison Avenue and Third Avenue and Second. At the end of a month, I hadn't found a pantsuit and the wedding was two weeks away. Then I went to an outlet store that sells cut-price designer clothes and found a grey satin pantsuit by Dior, beautifully simple, its only trim a small pink beaded emblem over the heart. But the suit was two sizes too big. I phoned Arlene and left a message on her answering machine, describing the suit and asking if her dressmaker could cut it down to fit me.

She phoned back the next morning.

"You can't cut a suit down two sizes!" she said tensely. "Forget it!"

"Well, I'm giving up!" I said, just as tensely. "There's nowhere left to look!" We hung up and I had hysterics. That was on a Sunday. At five p.m. on Monday Arlene phoned.

"It took me all day, but I found your pantsuit," she said. "It's a good thing you don't know how to shop; you'd have paid a fortune for it. You keep asking salesgirls; *they* don't know what's there! The girl at Bonwit's said they had nothing—and that's where I found it. It's a Calvin Klein, it's been in a corner on a sale rack for so long it was marked down four separate times! When I saw it was a size four, I had tears in my eyes."

It's turquoise, the blouse a high-necked Russian tunic, with small jet buttons on one shoulder and jet cuff links, and I look sensational in it.

We had one wedding rehearsal—over the phone.

"Go up to the hundred-and-seventh floor of the Trade Center and ask for the wedding room," said Arlene. "Go down and sit in the first seat in the first row on the right. When I reach the altar, get up and stand on my right."

Sitting there, I turned to see her come down the aisle and she looked beautiful, with pink and white flowers in her dark hair. She wore a long white skirt sprinkled with small grey leaves, and above the skirt—the little grey blouse with the pink emblem *I'd* have bought if they'd had my size. No wonder she'd sounded tense on the phone.

The wedding dinner was at flower-decked tables in a private room of Windows on the World. I can't tell you how I felt that evening. I think no matter how old you get, or how sophisticated you look, deep inside your head you're never more than twelve years old. Staring out at New York's incredible night sky from a festive private room in the city's most fabulous restaurant, I thought:

"How did a timid, awkward little girl from Philadelphia ever get *here*?" I never stop being awed at the incredible things that happen to me. Being Arlene's Maid of Honor was one of them.